Rimaletta Ray, Ph. D

I AM FREE TO BE THE BEST OF ME!

The Matrix of a Personality Formation

The Greatest Art of All is to Self-Install!

Copyright © 2019 by Dr. Rimaletta Ray.

ISBN   Softcover   978-1-950580-10-1

All rights reserved. No part of this book may be reproduced or transmitted in any form or by any means, electronic or mechanical, including photocopying, recording, or by any information storage and retrieval system without express written permission from the author, except in the case of brief quotations embodied in critical reviews and certain other non-commercial uses permitted by copyright law.

Printed in the United States of America.

To order additional copies of this book, contact:
Bookwhip
1-855-339-3589
https://www.bookwhip.com

Dedication

*To my dear grandson, **Mark Gazarkh**, and all those who are left fatherless too early in their lives, but who are growing spirit-fortified and unbeatable in **character-formation and self-realization**.*

My deepest and heartfelt gratitude to our Spiritual Philosophers:

Drunvalo Melchizedek, John Baines, Deepak Chopra, Osho, Dr. Fred Bell, Dr. Paul Pearsall, Dr. Wayne Dyer, Neale Donald Walsh, Daniel Goldman, Dr. John Hagelin, Dr. Mandelbrot, Sadhguru and many advanced thinking scientists that I quote a lot in my books.

I have the deepest respect for their wonderful minds and a valuable contribution to mine.

To All Those Who Do Not Live for a Pose,

and Who Love Life in its Entire Mass,

For It Too Shall Pass!

To Self-Excel,
Be the Best Version of Yourself!

Life in its Essence is Tenacity and Perseverance!

Will Your Life More! That's the Law!

Table of Content:

Foreword – **Unify the Soul and Consciousness as One!**----------------pp. 9-11

Book Rationale – **Choreograph Yourself Holistically!**--------------pp. 12-28

1. *For the Reader to Consider*
2. *Self-Perfection is the Way to Self-Resurrection!*
3. *Your Life is Your Making!*
4. *I am Teaching You to be Birds!*
5. *We are All the Lifelong learners of the Art of Living!*
6. *The Art of Living is the Art of Becoming!*
7. *Self- Actualization is in Personality Formation!*
8. *The Paradigm of Self-Resurrection*
9. *The Manuel of Life and Self-Creation*
10. *A Soul and Self-Consciousness in Synch*
11. *The Holistic Culture of Living*
12. *Shaping a Personality is the Demand of Time*
13. *To Be Inspired, Be Self-Inspiring!*
14. *Wow! I Live Now!*

Introduction – Cerebral Deprogramming----------------------------pp. 29-38

1. *Don't Take Life for Granted!!*
2. *Follow the Bliss of the Uncatchable "Is!"*
3. *Cerebral Deprogramming Today.*
4. *The Tree of Knowledge*
5. *You Are What You Sow!*
6. *I KnowWwho I Am!*

Part One – Holistic Methodology of Self-Creation (*Grains of Me and My Philosophy*)--pp. 39-51

1. *We are forming New Life Fractals!*
2. *Ascending Self-Consciousness*
3. *New Holistic" We - Concept"*
4. *Re-Invention of Self*
5. *The Hollstlc Life Paradigm*
6. *"Ignorance is the Worst Enemy of the Humanity!"*
7. *The Paradigm of a Personality Formation*
8. *Taming of the Inner Chaos*
9. *Death of Ignorance*
10. *Self-Emancipation is a Personality Salvation!*

Part Two – The Matrix of Personality Formation (*The Main Parts of the book start here*)---pp. 52-61

1. *The Ladder of Self-Resurrection*
2. *Personal Informational Field*

3. Step One – Upgrade Your Intelligence!
4. Step Two – Refine your Soul!
5. Step Three – Modify Your Personality!
6. Perform Self- Sculpturing without Fracturing!
7. The Matrix of Personality Formation

Part Three – Self-Knowledge *(The Physical Dimension of the Holistic Self-development)*--pp. 62-85

1. I Know Who I Am!
2. The Spiral of Self-Growth
3. Personality Development Ecology
4. Resist the Philosophy of Immediate Gratification!
5. Inner Dignity and Self-Identity
6. Insightful Self-Quest is Abreast!
7. Psychological Intelligence is a Must!
8. The Trajectory of Personality Formation
9. "The Best of Me!" Self-Image
10. "The Worst of Me!" Self-Image
11. Characteristics of an Advanced Soul
12. The Conceptual Hierarchy of the Ultimate Result Vision (URV)
13. The Basic Self-Induction for Self-Production
14. Stabilize Yourself!
15. Develop Love Intelligence without Negligence!
16. Sex without Love is a Bluff!
17. The Grid of Love-Consciousness
18. Be a Star! Love Yourself the Way You Aer!
19. Protect Your Solar System!
20. My Body is My Temple!
21. For the Reader to Consider

Part Four – Self-Monitoring *(The Emotional Dimension of the Holistic Self-Development)*--pp. 86-111

1. A True Savant is Constructively Self-Conscious
2. Being the Best is a Tough Test!
3. Self-Refinement is Mental First!
4. A Free Man is a Self-Sufficient One!
5. Reflective Thinking and Self-Scanning
6. Conscience Counseling
7. Self-Taming is the Main Personal Gaining!
8. Don't Rust from Lust!
9. 9.Love or Lust - Who Can I Trust?
10. Magnetization vs. De-magnetization
11. Spreading Love Magnetism
12. Emotional Self- Awareness
13. Language- Speech Awareness
14. Take Charge of Your Internal Pharmacy
15. Conduct a Self- Restriction War! Less is More!
16. Accumulating Personal Magnetism
17. Staying Young is a Life-Lasting Fun!

18. *Self-Infusion deletes Life's Confusion!321*
19. *Holistic Self- Scanning*
20. *Watch Your Mind's Torch!*
21. *For the Reader to Consider*

Part Five - Self-Installation *(The Mental Dimension of the Holistic Self-Development)*--pp. 112-130

1. *"Learning is not Outside; It's inside the Man!"*
2. *The Blueprint of Intellectual Self – Growth*
3. *Holistic Intelligence and Cycles of Personal Growth*
4. *You Need a Lot New Food for Thought!*
5. *Preserve Your Mental Sanity and Individuality!*
6. *Self-Efficacy is Intelligence Based!*
7. *Being Nice is a Holistic Device!*
8. *Compliments are Our Back Bones!*
9. *Moral Intelligence and Magnetism*
10. *The Path of Moral Maturity*
11. *Enact Your Endless Kindness Stream!*
12. *Connect the Heart and the Mind!*
13. *A Meditator is the Brain Sculptor!*
14. *Have a Meditative Test; Be the Best!*
15. *Be Self- Re- Assessing; not Soul-Recessing!*
16. *Live Consciously!*
17. *For the Reader to Consider*

Part Six – Self-Realization *(The Spiritual Dimension of the Holistic Self-Development)*--pp. 131-160

1. *"My Life is My Mission!"*
2. *Self-Realization without Frustration*
3. *Develop the Whole Brain!*
4. *Defy the Gravity of the Common Thought!*
5. *Sacred Territory of the Right hemisphere.*
6. *Creative Foundation of Self- Formation*
7. *The Holistic Culture of Ingenuity*
8. *Financial Awareness*
9. *Don't Let the Negative Stuff Occupy Your Mind's Gulf!*
10. *Be Self- Monitored, Not Society-Programmed!*
11. *Inertia of Thinking, Speaking, and Acting!*
12. *What's Yours is Limitless!*
13. *Professional Consciousness*
14. *Professional Self-Assessment*
15. *"Be the Thing in Itself!"*
16. *Professional Intelligence Auto-Suggestively*
17. *Infuse Your Self-Realization Fuse! (An Inspirational Booster)*
18. *Victory Over Yourself is Your Magic Spell!*
19. *I Am My Own Best Friend ! (Mental Trip One)*
20. *The Ultimate Picture of Me (Mental Trip Two)*
21. *I Can! I Want to! And I Will! (Mental Trip Three)*
22. *I Won't Go Afore; I'll Will My Life More! (Mental Trip Four)*

23. Self-Affirming is Character-Forming! (Mental Trip Five)
24. In My Life Quest, I Am the Best!
25. For the Reader to Consider

Part Seven – Self-Salvation *(The Universal Dimension of the Holistic Self-Development)*--pp. 161-181

1. Change Your Life's Algorithm to Self-Enthusiasm!
2. Becoming Spiritually- Aristocratic
3. Spiritual Maturation is our Self-salvation!
4. Spiritual Wellness is Wholeness
5. Stages of Wellness. are the Stages of Wholeness!
6. Spirituality is our Healing Modality!
7. "You Are Your Own Church!"
8. Spiritual Luminosity
9. Rationalize your Life – Thrive!
10. Intuition is the Mind's Fruition!
11. The Ultimate Result Vision of the Best of You
12. Envision a Better Scenario of Your Life – Thrive!
13. We are all in the Court of the Almighty God!
14. The Auto-Suggestive Meditation
15. I Never Whine; I Shine!
16. Make Your Heart Smart and Your Mind Kind!
17. Don't Be Life-Negligent; Be Life-Intelligent!
18. For the Reader to Consider

Conclusion - I Am Free; I Am the Whole Me!----------------------pp. 182-192

1. I am Flying Like an Angel!
2. Being the Best is a Life-Long Quest!
3. There are No Limits to Perfection!
4. The Vintage Me is All You Should See!
5. The Law of Reap and Sow is on the Go!
6. Final Self-Induction
7. Nothing is Impossible for Anyone Personable!

Post Thought – "Go Beyond, Fully Beyond, Completely Beyond!"

Individuate Yourself in Every Cell!

Build up Your Inner Fort with the Inspirational Word!

Foreword

"From the Relative Truth to the Absolute Truth!"

(John Baines)

To Unify the Soul and Consciousness as One is the Goal of Everyone!

**Don't Live on the Installment Plan,
Focus on the Self-Realization of Your Life Span!**

Epigraph

In My Exceptional Life!

In my exceptional life,

I manage to survive

Through every trouble and tribulation

With a sense of elation!

      How do I obtain

      This strength to sustain

      The test of the life's quest

      With a strong spiritual zest?

I guess my equation

Of pressure and pleasure

Comes in the bits of treasure

That only God can measure!

    Joy-ology is My Phycology!

Learn to Fly in Your Mind
And Be One of a Kind!
Life Needs to be Savored, not Endured!

*There is No Better Day
Than Today;
There is No Future,
No Past,
Only NOW to Last!*

*Nothing is Impossible for the One
who wants to Be Personable!*

Life is the Choice of Having a Personal Voice!

Book Rationale

Choreograph Yourself Holistically!

(The Know-How of Self-Creation)

**"Let Him Who Would Move the World
First Move Himself!"**

(Socrates)

Don't Be Bereft by the Chaos in Your Head! "

With a Self-Order Guide,
Internal Chaos Will Subside!

1. For the Reader to Consider

The book *"I Am Free to be the Best of Me!"* is presenting the self-creation process *in the initial physical dimension of the holistic self-creation process*, featuring consequentially the stages of **Self-Awareness, Self-Monitoring, Self-Installation, and Self-Realization**. Every stage, in turn, is viewed in five philosophical levels: ***physical, emotional, mental, spiritual, and universal*** consequentially, too. The Self-Resurrection process is crowning all five transformational stages from bottom to top integrally, following the holistic paradigm of thought-formation:

Synthesis-Analysis-Synthesis

There is no system without the structure!

The Holistic Self-Actualization Pyramid / Books, featuring these stages:

5. Universal level	Self-Salvation	" Beyond the Terrestrial!"
4. Spiritual level	Self-Realization	" Self-Taming!"
3. Mental level	Self-Installation	" Living Intelligence of the Art of Becoming!"
2. Emotional level	Self-Monitoring	" Soul-Refining!'
1. Physical level	Self-Awareness	" I Am Free to Be the Best of Me!"

The conceptual frame-work of all five books follows the structure of **the Russian Dolls,** Matryoshkas, when one level incorporates the next one, forming **one simple, holistic system of Self-Installation in life**, prompted by the present-day technological revolution and the necessity to adjust our personal pace to it, balancing between inner lie and goodness that prevails, but often fails.

The book presents the initial level of self-creation *in a holistic way* that helps a person develop his / her **new sense of identity**, the identity of the one with **"spiritualized intelligence,"** considerably **raised self-consciousness**, and the uncluttered **MIND + HEART** connection that are supposedly being developed by a reader in the creative process of self-transformation, led by the blue-print, presented in all five books as *the route of inspirational Self-Resurrection*.

I am here to pinpoint the way to self-change and self-growth, not as a dictator, but as an instructor who had verified this way with hundreds of her students that *got self-inspired and self-transformed with this vision installed.*

"The Life that is not Examined is not Worth Living!"

(Socrates)

2. Self-Perfection is the Way to Self-Resurrection!

The Universal Consciousness is ruling the World and You in it, too!

The Stages of Self-Growth:

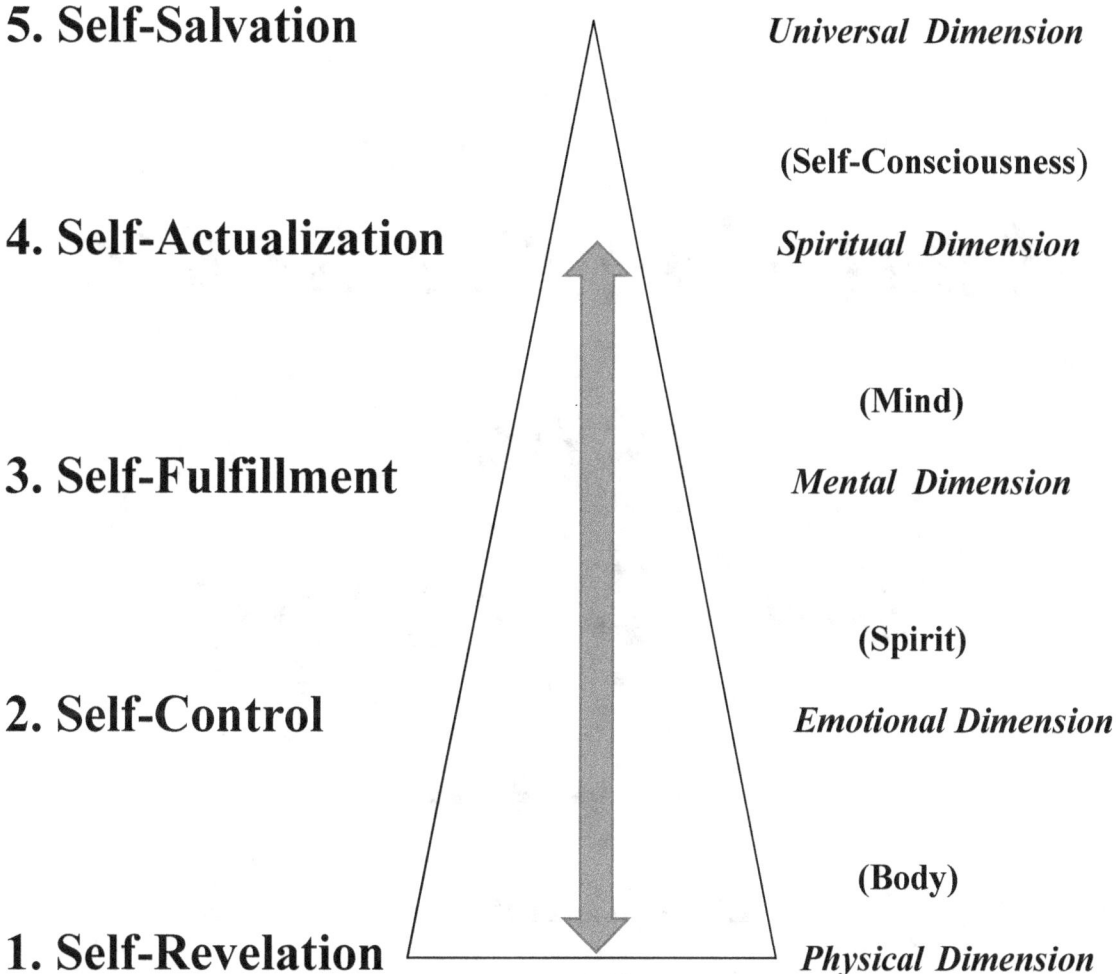

The Spiritual Fractals of Being:

Body + Spirit + Mind + Self-Consciousness + the Universal Consciousness = A Soul-Refined Self!

I am here to pinpoint the way of performing self-change and self-growth, not as a dictator, but as an instructor who had verified this way with hundreds of students that got self-inspired and self-transformed with this vision installed.

Tame your analytical thinking to give visual thinking a chance!

Self-Salvation is in Our Spiritual Maturation!

3. "Your Life is Your Making!"
(Sadhguru)

Learning the Route is just the First Step!

Continuing the **SELF-CREATION** journey depends on complying with the <u>**MIND + SPIRIT + HEART + SELF-CONSCIOUSNESS + THE UNIVERSAL CONSCIOUSNESS**</u> created connections and establishing the individually- followed procedures!

"Learning is Remembering and Following!" *(Plato)*

4. I Am Teaching You to Be Birds!

(An Inspirational Booster)

I am teaching you to be birds
And to fly in your mind's outskirts

To conquer the unreachable skies
And to be unapproachable for human flies

To establish a personal Verizon
And to outline your own horizon!

To come up with an invention
In a new, unthinkable dimension

And to roam the skies
Beyond the terrestrial ties!

" *The light is too painful for someone who wants to remain the darkness!" (Eckhart Tolle)*

Learn to Fly in your Mind;
Be One of a Kind!

5. We are All Lifelong Learners of the Art of Living!

The technological revolution, largely sustained by a new digital era, is the core of human evolution now, and it is just as profound for our educational system today as the Internet revolution was 20 years ago. The potentialities of this new educational tool are defining a new approach to knowledge acquisition, career building opportunities, and, most importantly, to **a personal growth.** Thanks to the tools of science, we now know that *"personality is more complex and beautiful than previously believed.* ("National Geographic", Your personality, July,2017)

Our new technological make-up and its informational demands are changing ***the content*** and ***the form of our education*** and promoting the necessity for self-education and self-creation. The process of information processing and its fundamental enrichment with the latest developments in science, or mega-science, changes the scene of today's brutally competitive world. To adjust to it, education needs to become ***systemic and holistic,*** prioritizing intelligence, consciousness raising, soul-refining, and personality formation because technology is not only expanding our intellectual horizons, it is also democratizing our knowledge of life and ourselves

However, we know that, but we are not aware of that!

Awareness of the newest developments in different fields of knowledge and, especially, in brain science is essential for us now because life becomes tougher, and our personal adjustment to its fast pace and exponential growth needs to be even tougher. In other words, education should become vertical, giving way to a person's ***early self-discovery***, ***creative self-expression,*** and ***full self-realization*** within the life time. We need to re-appreciate life and our place in it. The Art of Living should be studied by us along the holistic paradigm: ***Synthesis-Analysis-Synthesis***. *(See "The Holistic Methodology of Self-Creation, Part One"),*

Internalizing – Personalizing – Externalizing!

The problems that we must solve today are not only political, economic, educational; they are ***holistic and universal!*** Under the pressure of the electronic evolution, our personal DNA is rapidly changing, making holistic development and raising of consciousness our common goal. Most importantly, we need to develop a new level of ***personal maturation,*** based on *"spiritualized intelligence"* *(Dr. Fred Bell)* and exponential development of ***self-consciousness.***

"New Times are the times of Exponential Learning!"

(Ray Kurzweil)

6. The Art of Living is the Art of Becoming!

In my first book of the trilogy on a personality formation geology, of which this one is the third, called *"Living Intelligence or the Art of Becoming,"* I call upon scientists and educators to come up with

THE MANUEL OF LIFE and **SELF – CREATION.**

Such Manuel is meant to help our kids and college students become more informed and better focused on *self-installation in life* first and getting a materialistically-successful career next. A shift in thinking should be instilled in their minds - *from having to being and becoming!* As Leo Vygotsky, a great Russian psychologist, killed by Stalin during his repressions, writes, *"When a person knows his mission on earth, he lives most purposefully and effectively. The life without a purpose of self-creation is pointless."*

The present day exponential growth of technology and the avalanche of information that overwhelms us demand that we channel our intelligence along the path of full personal *self-realization* and spiritual *self-salvation.*

Before you can get something, you must become somebody!

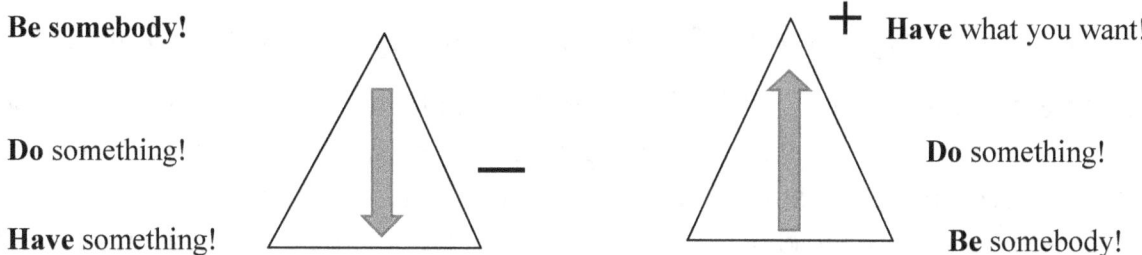

Having helps, no doubt about it, but it doesn't shape your personality intellectually, spiritually, and universally. Having must be the result of the changed life paradigm, when a person achieves a sure *self-installation* and *full self-realization* in life in synch with the material reward.

"Income rarely exceeds personal development!" (Reid Hoffman)

In our psychological make-up, we are all the result of the past, but the product of the present. We do not develop just in a linear way now, focusing on the benefits of a well-chosen professional field and career accomplishments that guarantee a decent material life in the future. Starting a career and even accomplishing it is not the destination anymore!

A New Personality of Holistic Intelligence, a Free Spirit, and Character are needed now!

7. Self-Actualization is in Personality Formation!

Life demands self-perfection during life time and full self-realization of our mission on earth at its outcome. In his book, *"Psychology of Art"*, Leo Vygotsky reiterates the idea of self-realization in life and" the **necessity to become a personality in it"** as the pivotal one in psychology.

"Psychology exists for one purpose only – to shape you into a personality!"

Without accomplishing *self-actualization* in life, no one can be completely happy and have no regrets about aimlessly lived life. Each of us is the key person in his / her life, and it is worth every treasure on earth to better oneself and to do what we are sculptured for by the **Universal Informational Field**, the Magnetic Circuit of Life, or the Master Mind that we call God.

"The personality is a unique roleplay of the mind!" (Leo Vygotsky)

On the path of a passionate self-expression, your **heart and mind will get in synch**, and being kind, responsive, compassionate, loving and caring will not seem to be hard to obtain. It will come naturally to you, if you believe in yourself and keep moving forward toward full accomplishment of your unique mission in life - *the realization of the God-given gift of self-creation!* Albert Einstein said,

"Life is like riding a bicycle. To keep your balance, you must keep moving."

People will gravitate to you! Your personal magnetism will charge them, and your inner light will illuminate your life and theirs, leaving the marks of your soul light's accomplishments as your legacy to the next generations. Everyone has a free will to choose whether to create himself / herself and live a meaningful, intellectually and spiritually mature life of true human quality or to go with the flow of "**the dysfunctional civilization** *(Al Gore),* "**collective unconscious**" *(Carl Yung),* or *the* common crowd, *busy* with money-chasing and *immediate* gratification whims. Life is a form of transformation that starts and ends in us.

"The choices we make dictate the life we live!"

More particularly, the paradigm for a constructive self-creation has changed dramatically, and it, works only in one way –

First, become someone, do something, and then you will have something!

In sum, only an accomplished, ***personable, spiritually-mature*** human being with the mind-set like that will have every right to declare,

I am Free to Be the Best of Me!

8. The Paradigm of Self-Resurrection

There is a common opinion that wealth gives class, grace, and stature. Wealth surely helps, but ***a great personality and wealth go together*** only when being a great person, you are doing what only you can do. A person becomes unbeatable on the way of self-realization because he / she gets charged from the Above with ***the spirit of a winner,*** sure of the absolute correctness of his ideas that he channels in the direction that the Universal Informational Field is pointing out to him.

It does not work in a reverse way because the reverse way does not develop a person's SELF-CONSCIOUSNESS! The other way is the dead end that does not make a person self-realized spiritually and obtain ***"spiritualized intelligence"*** (*Dr. Fred Bell*) that propels a person to the stars because he can defy the gravity of the common.

Those who defy – fly; those who crawl -die!

The result is always the same, according to the British philosopher David Eike: ***"We have giants of money and intellect, but "pigmies of spiritual qualities."***

Only, developing self-consciousness can you obtain true spiritual maturity, personal integrity, and charismatic magnetism that are the prerequisites of ***high self-consciousness*** that must be the outcome of any one's life. Only having developed high self-consciousness, can you expand your personal informational field and get connected to ***the Universal Informational Field,*** or *"The Source"* (*Dr. Wayne Dyer*) The paradigm of self- creation goes like this:

Body + Spirit+ Mind+ Self-Consciousness + Super-Consciousness

= Self- Creation!

(Physical, emotional, mental, spiritual, and universal levels of personality-formation).

Thus, thanks to such holistic personal growth, you will be able to charge ***the Magnetic Circuit*** of your life, generated by your biological computer - your mind which, as science has it, is" ***an electrical device".*** This device needs to be charged intelligence-wise and become spiritually-mature to develop your own AUTO-MEDIA - ***your perceptive antenna*** to better receive the information from the Above, for, as the ancient Hermetic rule of life states,

"As it is above, so it is below!" As you think, so you are!

Only then will we be able to interpret and COOPERATE with the New Reality of life – THE DIGITAL REALITY!

You Need to Create Your Fate!

9. The Manuel Life and Self-Creation

Millennia of philosophy taught us many intellectually-exhilarating theories about the external life, and there are wonderful books on physiology and psychology that explore our inner world. However, the greatest discoveries in neuro-science and new biology are beyond the reach of our kids and life entering students.

We still lack the knowledge of ***the Science of Life,*** or ***the Art of Living*** that should, in fact, be the main subject of our education. The Art of Living is urgently needed to build up the core of our understanding how to handle life with all its twists and turns and, most importantly, with its digital make-up to develop our own auto-receptive device - ***the auto- media*** of the connection with the Source.

The first step to self-change is a new self- awareness!

I think that new philosophers, educators, psychologists, and cutting-edge neuroscientists should unite their expertise to produce ***the Manuel of Life and Self -Creation.*** The urgent necessity for us to study life and living by embracing it as one, interconnected, ever changing scientific phenomenon remains unmet. The stream of our consciousness doesn't go with the flow of the evolution. ***We are lagging in self-formation***, and we still do not know how to enjoy our time on Earth, irrespective of any problems that all of us face. As Dr. Bruce Lipton, a great scientist and an ardent advocate of conscious biology puts it,

"We need to change the Biology of Belief!"

Life demands that we change our focus from the known to the unknown and acquire ***the holistic level of life-awareness,*** rationalizing our lives and charging the personal informational field around us consciously to become better connected to the Universal Informational Field that is managing our lives. We just need to become ***better managers of ourselves*** to achieve a new level of personal freedom.

Dr. Bruce Lipton calls this new level of life-awareness about our biological and mental make-up ***"informational medicine."*** He states that our digitally-educated idea of ourselves makes us change the limited view that we are victims of a hereditary DNA. Dr. Lipton believes that genes are not responsible for our personalities and lives, but our programming of ourselves is. My understanding of the personality formation, therefore, goes beyond the accepted view that personality traits are a given. I adhere to Leo Vygotsky's view,

"You become a personality if you work on your self-creation!"

We are the Co-Creators of Life!

10. Soul and Self-Consciousness in Synch

Vygotsky is not talking here about a personality as a psychological type, but about ***a personality as a human being with a capital "H".*** We are the products of our intelligence, and therefore, we can be the masters of our minds, bodies, and lives, that are being programmed according to the information that is transmitted to our cells. *(Dr. Bruce Lipton)* and that we need to process intelligently, having acquired a new awareness of the reality that is digital now. Thus, we can assume that we are getting plugged to **the Magnetic Circuit of life** that needs another level of our souls' spiritual charge. Allow me to repeat the hermetic formula again,

"As it is Above, so it is below!

As we think, speak, feel, and act, so we are, or

As it in in the mind, so it is in the body!

The life of a person on earth will become much more meaningful and happier if we educate our souls and enrich them with **enlightened self-consciousness**. A new channel of evolutionary creation will be enacted in us then. So, each one of us has ***to develop his / her personal level of consciousness*** and ***personal auto-media***, a perceptive device to be able to tune to the Super-Mind of creation, God ,by establishing the unity of:

Body + Spirit + Mind+ Self-Consciousness + Super-Consciousness = Your Soul!

It's a challenging road that is demanding a lot of self-discipline and spiritual maturity before this channel is opened to most us. As a matter of fact, many spiritually and intellectually-advanced people on Earth have this line of connection and thanks to their exceptional in-put, we are developing in the right direction. The right direction relates to the right brain development that is the source of creation in the brain. It will be activated to a new level of functioning. The one who discovers the inner source of creativity by having put ***his soul*** and ***self- consciousness in synch*** is a truly happy person who reaches the stage of full real-realization and self-salvation.

This is what this book is all about.

Only the holistic connection between the heart and mind, or the soul and self-consciousness, that is broken at present can provide us with new life-awareness and give us inner strength and spiritual maturity. Then, the souls of those who can digest such symbiosis mentally and use it constructively will be able to change themselves and the world around them.

The history of the humanity has a lot of stories about such exceptional human beings, who "gave the world the best they had," and many of them are living among us now. But there are no shortcuts in achieving this transformation because **"the hardest job on Earth is the job at oneself!"** *(Delia Lama)* You must be willing to do this by stretching the mind's outfit and enlarging the volume of your soul.

We need to change the" izm" of the self- development algorism!

Obviously, pessimism, chauvinism, racism, and nationalism should be deleted from our souls, and a holistic optimism and intellectualism about the future of our wonderful planet need to be installed into the minds of the new generations.

In sum**, the Art of Becoming** requires our conscious reprogramming of selves to create Living Intelligence with an individual label for each of us.

To survive we need to study a new culture of life!

I have outlined this algorithm in the first two books on personality development *"Living Intelligence and the Art of Becoming"* and *"Soul Refining!"* They present the ways of self-creation in five levels: **physical, emotional, mental, spiritual, and universal,** and these are the levels that this book is built on, too.

Obviously, we absolutely need to make our overall education a real motivator *for* **conscious self-sculpturing** of our lives in these levels from as early age as possible. As a matter of fact, Vygotsky's view on personality formation has been the beacon of mine all my professional life. Both Vygotsky and another role model of mine, Carl Yung, who stressed the willful part of a man's life, too, helped me become what I am professionally and personality-wise myself, and thanks to them, I have managed to inspire hundreds of my students to get on **the path of self- installation** and stay on it for the rest of their lives.

"Don't teach just the subject, teach the whole person!" (Leo Vygotsky)

Learn to support your wishes with the help of the irresistible moves of your soul. Stay always connected to it!

A New, Personable You is a Better Aware You!

11. The Holistic Culture of Living!

Life demands that we apply the accumulated experience of the past to adjust self-development to the present to become better, younger, smarter, more self-accomplished people of the future. A holistically-developed person who has a great outlook, adjusts his attitude, and puts a smile on his face is in demand now. According to Albert Einstein,

"To be happy is to appreciate the time that you have and the space you are in.

As a matter of fact, happiness is directly connected to spirituality that is now acknowledged to be a scientific phenomenon. It is not just being religious, it is obtaining **the spirit that should be manifested through one's brain and the soul in a holistic unity.** To accomplish that we, need to adopt the holistic culture of living. New science sees **consciousness as the informational field of a person**, connected to the Universal Informational Field. Consequently, every human being should develop the ability to enrich his / her personal informational field and to obtain **spiritual maturity** that determines who he / she will become in life.

How your brain is wired determines how you are!

More particularly, spiritual maturity means becoming responsible for your own **personal evolution** that determines the level of your self-consciousness which, in turn, is manifested in your reflective reactions to the world and the ability to rationalize your perception of it.

Each of us needs **to turn on his / her auto-media device** to become auto-suggestively more perceptive and more able to connect to the Universal Mind and get to the next evolutionary stage. In the future, according to Steve Howkins and Ray Kurzweil, we'll be **"the hybrid of biological and technological intelligence"**, or our intelligence will merge with artificial intelligence. So, we absolutely need to monitor our response to the world holistically and consciously!

Next, to make yourself whole is to expand your knowledge of yourself and develop the will-power to be able to equip yourself with **a unique know-how of handling yourself, or acquiring true self-management.** *(See Part Three)*

Everyone's mission on Earth is to disarm the harm in oneself and in others with personal light and God-given might. Reid Hoffman, a great entrepreneur of the Silicon Valley and the founder of LinkedIn, defining such necessity of self-formation in his wonderful book *"The Start-Up of You"*. writes,

"Be Your Own Coach in Life! Become a Superior You!"

12. Shaping a Personality is the Demand of Time

In view of the above stated outlook, *the key goal of this book is to help you shape yourself into a personality,* a human being of a great personal integrity and magnetism. It is my modest attempt to present the blueprint of a holistic personality development as I see it, having shaped hundreds of my students into very successful, accomplished people, ready "to give the world the best they have." I think that personal growth goes far beyond gaining professional intelligence and satisfying career aspirations.

Self-actualization and self-installation are in focus now!

A substantial self-growth is an urgent demand of our technological times. We are going up the scale now, and to become more evolved means going with the flow of the evolution that is uplifting our self-consciousness and making us intellectually-spiritualized human beings that are on the path of becoming" *the Star people."* (*John Baines*)

Character-formation and self-realization are at the forefront of our economy.

We need leaders, not just managers, and leaders must be shaped and raised. On our present day evolutionary path, we are learning to transform the messages of the Universal Informational Field into our new reality which is, in fact, a *holographic matrix* of the Universal Mind. We are trying to intelligently connect to it and start experiencing ourselves as *free parts of the whole.*

What a breath-taking project that is, and we are its co-creators!

I hope that the ideas, presented in the three books of the trilogy and the inspirational self-inductions, illustrating them, will help you reach an internal. holistic equilibrium of the best of you state.

In my life quest, I am the best!

But such self-creation needs inspiration! So, I'd like to inspire you with the desire to see yourself as a unique mini-universe, that is part of the whole - the Universal Intelligence, governing the life on earth. So, start the process of molding and re-molding yourself to accomplish the happiness of full self-realization in life. New scientific discoveries show that consciousness affects matter, and the higher our consciousness is, the better connected to the Universal Intelligence we become. The auto-suggestive work that I am promoting will help you establish this line of connection consistently and consciously.

Self-Induction Boosts Self-Production!

13. To Be Inspired, Be Self-Inspiring!

The basic five levels of self-installation in life, as I see them - *physical, emotional, mental, spiritual, and universal* comprise, correspondingly, **the conceptual structure of five main parts of this book and its thesis,** and they are meant to channel your thinking and emotional make-up along the path of a very effective self-creation that had inspired very many of my students. You will easily work out your own modifications of these steps, **customizing them to your own personal needs**. Your obvious uniqueness and exceptionality determine your choices in life and the priorities that you single out for yourself. Sameness happens, however, repeatedly with little deviation from the commonly-accepted norms of thinking and behavior that bury our uniqueness then and there.

Don't compete and don't compare! Be unique here and there!

In all my books, I am continuously writing about the most beneficial effect of **Auto -Suggestive Psychology** for self-creation. I love the inspirational message of the book, *"Superjoy"* by Dr. Paul Pearsall. I found it lying on the ground among many other old, dirty books that were being sold by a street seller in Manhattan on the third day of my immigration to the USA from Latvia. In the turmoil of my life then, it was a ray of hope that remains so till this day. That's the psychology that I follow my auto-suggestive messages.

"Joyology" is my Psychology!

In my case, I suggest inducting the mind with **the rhyming inspirational** and **psychologically-charged boosters** and **mind-sets** (*authoritative commands to the mind here.*) because rhyming ideas get better stored in the brain and easier come to the mind when it's most needed to boost the spirit and add some emotional gas to a sagging psyche. To change yourself, you need to **AUTHORITATIVELY CHANGE YOUR THINKING** to enhance your connection to the Universal Intelligence through your **AUTO-MEDIA**. *(See above).* Thus, you will become a true master of your subconscious mind that will follow your conscious commands and channel you to self- actualization in the right direction.

I conclusion, let me remind you to preserve your uniqueness and exceptionality by using **the self-inductions** that are meant to be instilled in your sub-conscious mind and imbue you with an unbreakable desire **to reveal the Best of You**! You will not be overloaded with the redundant information. Every chapter in the book is **a page long** and is rounded off with the conceptually-unifying self-induction. As Edgar Cayce puts it,

"The Rhyming Word goes Better Inward!"

14. Wow! I Live now!

Life is a miracle

That can't be stopped

with a sigh;

Long live

the amplitude –

Either you fall or fly!

Remember, water never goes under the lying stone;
it goes around it.

Inspirational Auto-Induction is

the Onto-Genesis of Self-Production!

Introduction

Cerebral Deprogramming and Reprogramming, devoid of Whining!

Self-Sufficiency is True Self-Programming!

The Inner Dignity of the Whole is the Aristocratism of My Soul!

Carpe Diem!
Seize the day! Develop Your Auto-Media Today!

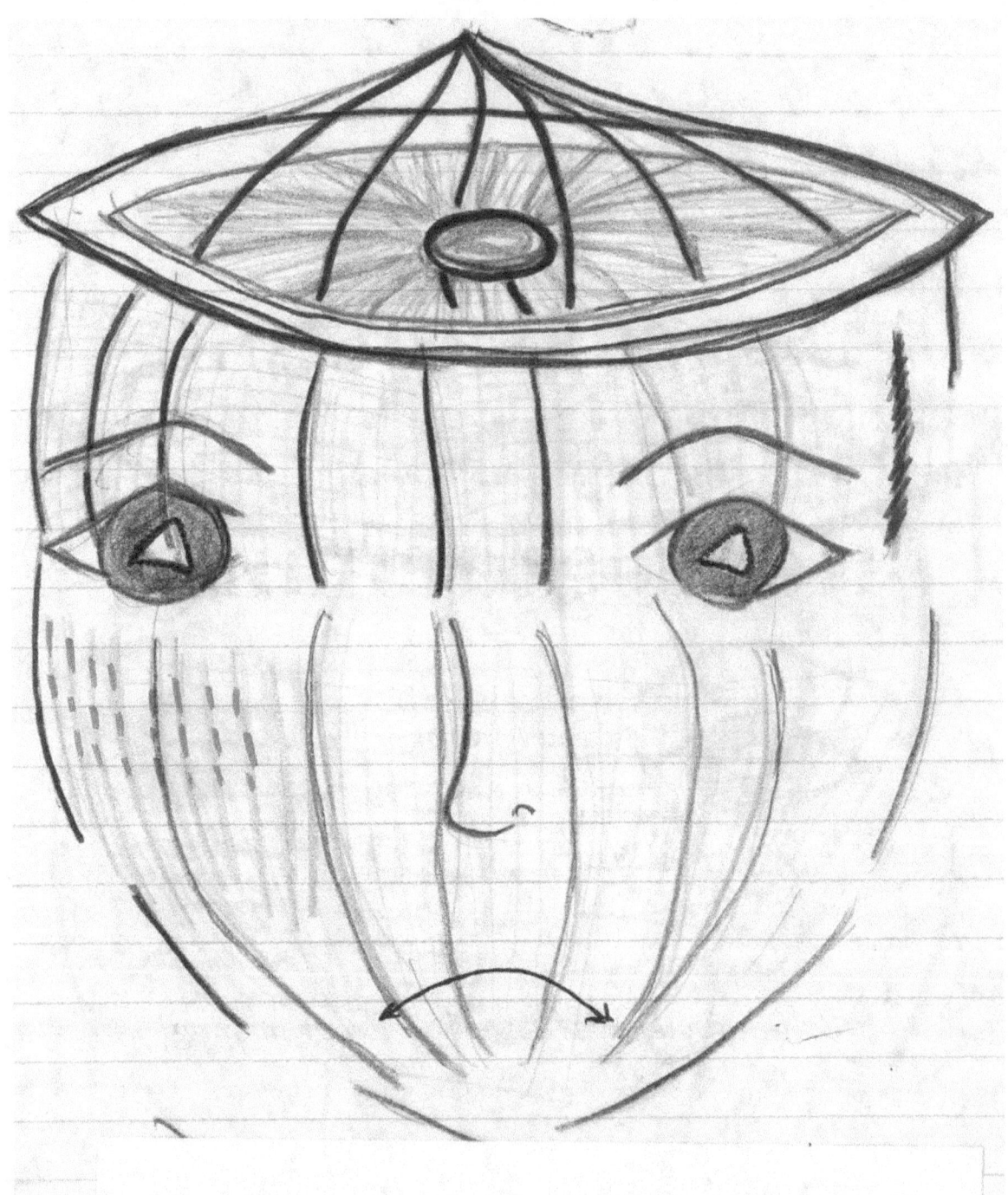

"Apply Your Heart to Instruction
and Your Mind to the Words of Wisdom"

(Proverb 22,12)

1. Don't Take Life for Granted;

***To Live and to Be Happy,
You Need
Just Two Things –
To Live and
To Be Happy!***

" Smiling and laughing are ways of voluntarily giving your brain an oxygen shower.

("Joylogy" by Dr. Paul Pearsall)

It is God Granted!

2. Follow the Bliss of the Uncatchable" Is!

Make your mind
    Feel
And the heart per-
    ceive
               The power of
                "Is"
                In its revealing
                Bliss!

Plug into the void
    Inside You,
Feel the sacredness
    Of "Is,"
                Learn the power of
                Now
                To appreciate life
                AS IS!

The work of the mind or true intelligence
resists aging and life-negligence!

Our Human Essence is in Spiritual Renaissance!

3. Cerebral Deprogramming Today

We absolutely need *to prioritize human identity and exceptionality,* intellect and wisdom, empathy and oneness with the Mother Nature, love and peace, de facto, not de juror, starting with **monitoring ourselves** consciously and continuously. Let's stop justifying disrespect, humiliation, racism, injustice, ignorance, absence of emotional intelligence, and crime that generate unwanted friction in life.

"Injustice anywhere is a threat of justice everywhere." (M. L. King, Jr)

Let's also bless our intelligent and spiritually-advanced people who illuminate the world with their presence in it. We have a great number of wonderfully ingenious people in the USA, and they come from all over the world, raising the world's consciousness and tapping the Universal Informational field to make us the Star people of the future. As the ancient Hermetic philosophy holds, it cannot be achieved *"without a substantial human effort".*

"A man is a micro-cosmos of the Universe. So, to get to know the Universe, you need to know yourself first."

Hopefully, we'll have more of knowledgeable and thought-provoking programs on TV that would help our young minds steer themselves along the path of self-creation, imbuing them with an unbeatable spirit to achieve it.

You can roam any terrain with an unbreakable spirit in your vein!

Unfortunately, unconscious patterns of behavior dominate now. People are driven by the psychology of the masses when *"he is not the individual himself, he is a robot who has no will."* Le Ron), The rust of destruction is rapidly absorbing our daily lives and stealing away our badly needed free time to the point that all we can do is to listlessly absorb the TV most intellectually-debilitating shows. Even the news is full of cooking debates. As a result, we hardly have any energy for a face-to-face, mind-to-mind, and heart–to heart communication with anybody.

Mind-to mind and heart-to-heart disconnection is ruling the world!

To illuminate this disconnection, holistic personal revolution, performed by everyone, interested in self-evolution is needed. It should be based on better awareness about life and self and holistic thinking, connecting our **physical, mental, verbal, emotional, psychological, professional, cultural, social, and spiritual** fundamentals of life. *(See the book" Living Intelligence or the Art of Becoming!)*

Science has it that our intelligence / consciousness is part of the dynamic Universe and its *Universal Informational Field.* A human being is an expression of consciousness; he is not independent. He is intellectually and spiritually channeled through life by the Universal Mind. Humanity is on a spiritual journey, the destination of which is the unification with God, or *"obtaining spiritualized intelligence which means uniting with the Divine." (Dr. Fred Bell)*

The inspirational **AUTO-SUGGESTIVE METHODOLOGY FOR SELF-ECOLOGY** presented in this book is meant to help you do that. With the help of the auto-suggestively installed **AUTO-MEDIA**, a sharpened self-perception of reality, **YOUR GOD-ATTUNED INTUITION**, you will have a chance to enhance your immense creativity, expand your *"spiritualized intelligence"*, and develop high, **DIGITALLY-ENHANCED** self-consciousness.

We are here to discover ourselves!

The religious paradigm that the humanity has been following for centuries has contributed a lot to our spiritual growth, but *we have come to the point of no return in it* because our religious differences are blinding us and pushing our personal growth to stagnation, stereotyped thinking, and dogmatic judgment.

It is paramount now to reassess the reality in the light of the acquired religious wisdom together with new scientific developments.

In other words, we need to connect our piety-filled hearts with technologically-advanced minds. Disconnection is the action of entropy, or the reflection of death!

A lot of intellectual and spiritual brewing must be done without sewing!

In sum, the holistic personal evolution that I am talking about here is often side-tracked or neglected while it should be based on holistic awareness of the true realities of life and self and backed up with the **SCIENCE OF LIFE**.

Let's Reprogram our Brains Without Any Vanity, from Religiousness to Spirituality!

4. The Tree of Knowledge

New, holistic awareness of how our life gets processed in time and space becomes an urgent necessity, and an indispensable life mode by which every one of us should be consciously steering oneself to full self–actualization *as the demand of our time.* There are many incredible philosophies, starting with the antient Hermetic and Kabalistic ones, that educate us how to move along *the Tree of Knowledge* to complete our spiritual mission as a valuable leaf on *the Tree of Life.* All sacred books that has the Word of God teach us the universal wisdom.

"If we achieve the change of consciousness, we'll be able to enlighten the dark corridors of our lives." (Rev. PS. Berg)

We know the ancient wisdom, but we do not follow it. Obviously, our perception has changed over the centuries. We have developed a new belief system, and we need to adjust our Three of Knowledge to a new reality, never forgetting the greatest accomplishments of the past. As Don Miguel Ruiz says,

"Each of us has his own tree of knowledge which is our own belief system."

Each of us writes his / her own book of life, chapter by chapter. Each book has **the starting point** at birth. Then a person is processing his life through its plot development around many conflicts between life and death, energy and entropy. **The culminating point** comes in the middle of the life story with the resolution of the conflict inevitably coming next, and, finally, a person rounds off his life story with **the conclusion** of the life cycle. **The Catharsis,** or the realization of the outcome of life, is to be experienced by each of us, too, and this is the main stage of our lives that comes with the last breath of either gratitude or regret.

This universal orderliness rules your life!

So, be spiritually-fit ; get in touch with it!

We are all yarning for life contentment, for more self-recognition, for something that our souls long for. But we must reject a lot of ignorance that puts our consciousness out of its conceptual form. As Leo Vygotsky writes, *"We develop the soul and the spirit forces through only a well-educated, self-made man, able to accomplish full self-realization and become a personality."* Only developing intelligence in the essential areas of life, working on self-creation and self-actualization can you satisfy your hunger for full self-realization in life and obtain" ***soul's resurrection."*** *(Dr. F. Bell)*

Holistic Self-Reflection leads to Self-Resurrection!

5. You Are What You Sow!

The world is full of unhappy people that seek to satisfy their internal hunger for the solution of daily problems and get the answer to the question,

What am I here for?

To answer this question, we need to take the side of light in life and stay there, by charging ourselves physically, emotionally, mentally and spiritually.

Overpower the evil and become more civil!

The problem is we need ***a strategic plan of action***, or ***the blueprint of self-creation***, on the one hand, and an individualized recipe for each disturbed soul, on the other, the soul that needs a lot of self-enrichment, will-power, perseverance, self-respect, and self-realization.

You need to sow new, holistic seeds of life to thrive!

Unfortunately, most of us spend lives bouncing back and forth between the good and evil of life. It wears out our souls and deplete us of the spirt of self-formation. Rabbi P. S. Berg, the author of a very wisdom-generating book "***Taming Chaos,***" writes that we can tame the three beasts that get us into the disbalance (***mind*** + ***heart*** + ***sex***) only if we put them under the control of the conscious mind. His Kabalistic philosophy calls on us to establish order in life and reverse the life from the disbalance of **666** *(the symbol of evil and death)* to **999** *(the symbol of life)*

To be one of the best life cells - Conquer Yourself!

The present-day science claims that we can throw the Earth's hemostasis out of balance due to our ***backward thinking***! Apparently, everyone needs MUCH **MORE LIFE AWARENESS** and individualized food for thought that will feed the broken spirit because every one of us has a traumatized spirit due to having been exposed to life's unavoidable day-to-day test of being fit for taking sides in the fight of intelligence against ignorance or good against evil. Very beautiful and fair words by Al Gore immediately come to mind here:

"There is an invisible war on the planet.
We. as a dysfunctional civilization, are in this war, too. We need to take sides! The question is which one?"

We are governed by the Universal Laws of life that shape us irreversibly and make us answer the question above this way or the other. The Law of Sow and Reap, the Law of Cause and Effect, and the Law of Gravity are the core universal laws that we must follow on the path of self-creation. ***The Law of Sow and Reap*** is the fundamental spiritual law of life - construction that is to be considered first.

Our thoughts are seeds and the mind is the fertilized soil

that produces the crops.

Undoubtedly, our parents initially create and shape our personal world. We get the inherited traits of character and the ones, formed by them, and we continue ***shaping our own personalities ourselves*** till the rest of our lives. People live their lives with either no regrets, or they waste their lives because no self-realization was accomplished.

So, the mission of self-salvation was not completed!

The Law of Sow and Reap is directly connected ***to the auto-inductive work*** that all my books are based on. Every chapter in this book, ends with a self-induction of ***an inspirational, mind-sowing character*** that generalizes the concept of the chapter.

Strengthen your personal gene with self-suggestive hygiene!

I am sure that you have noted by now that almost every paragraph, or a set of paragraphs in the chapters are concluded with the mind-sets of an inductive character. Such self-inducting is meant to boost your spirit and strengthen the determination to stay on the self-installation path.

If your thoughts are constructive on the track of self-creation, you will sow the most personable changes in yourself!

Evolved thoughts always give a boost to evolved, reasoned out actions that are governed by the Universal Intelligence and perceived by you thanks to your developing ***auto-media*** of the holistic life observation and its realistic, intellectually-spiritualized perception. Be sure to install in the mind the self-inductions below:

The Purity of My Intention is of the Highest Dimension!

I am Becoming a Much Wiser Self-Actualizer!

6. I Know Who I Am!

The Main Auto-Induction:

I'm a Strong, Calm, and Determined Owner of My Firm Will!

I Can be the Best I am!
I Want to be the Best I am!
I Will Be the Best I am!

Tools of Creation are in the Aware Life-Reflection!

Part One

Holistic Methodology of Self-Creation

(Grains of Me and My Philosophy)

Before Saying, "I Can Do It," You Need to Know How to Do It!

1. We are Forming New Life Fractals!

The individualized vision of life comes with full awareness. To be able to apply the holistic paradigm to life, presented above *(Rationale, Ch. 9, 10)*, we need to have more awareness of life and appreciate its present, or **"to live in the Now**" *(Eckhart Tolle)* consciously, continuously, and religiously.

When you are in the present, it becomes the present of God!" (Neale D. Walsch)

Understanding of life comes through awareness. Awareness means to be aware of life" *as is"* at this moment without any judgement with full acceptance of the gift of life that yet needs to be unwrapped and appreciated.

Freeing the spirit and raising the consciousness is everyone's individual responsibility now. It must be instilled in the minds and hearts of our children as early as possible through personality development. Developing ourselves, we are learning to live by *mind + heart* indivisible unity that our inner barometer - *conscience / intuition* tunes us to, making our lives godlier, more conscientious, considerate, full of faith, and love.

Make your heart smart and the mind kind; be one of a kind!

Unfortunately, the future of our human souls does not seem to be promising in view of the accelerating development of cold, inhuman intelligence that lacks spiritual insightfulness.

Due to high tech explosion, life has a different narrative of self-erosion.

There is also another reason for which self-development is extremely timely to be paid extra attention to now. Unfortunately, the time of an unprecedented socialization of our lives **pollutes us in the core and demands ecological attempts** on our part to be doubled in soul refining effort. There is order and harmony in the Universal Super Intellect that is everywhere and that we are part of, but that we are disturbing with our "*collective unconscious.*" *(Carl Yung)*

So, I am claiming in my second book of the trilogy "*Soul Refining!*" that it is paramount for us to refine our souls because **we are forming new**, **holistic life fractals** now, fractals being the main structures of nature, discovered by a phenomenal mind, an IBM scientist and professor of mathematics in Yale, *Benoit B. Mandelbrot*.

Following **Dr. Mandelbrot's discovery**, I think that we are forming our life-fractals, too. Our new, holistic life fractals are now acquiring a new function in the circuitry of digitally-spiritualized life energy.

We are generating a New Life Symmetry in us!

2. Ascending Self-Consciousness

Life fractals are formed at birth, and they encapsulate our souls that are first developed by our parents. They open our hearts and minds to God by introducing us to the religious paradigm. of their spiritual choice. While we are growing spiritually, it is each one's personal goal t*o develop his / her own paradigm of spiritual maturation.* We are responsible to turn our religious make-up into a highly spiritual and personable one on the path of making it universal. That's why I think that the philosophy of *mind+ body* that was so brilliantly introduced by Deepak Chopra, a great philosopher of our time, needs to be enriched with a holistic one, as a holistic paradigm of self-development, mentioned above.

Our Life -Being / Creating Fractals:

Body+ Spirit + Mind + Self-Consciousness + Super-Consciousness

(The line of connection with the Universal Mind)

In other words, this paradigm presents the holistic unity of the *physical, emotional, mental, spiritual, and universal* levels of our evolutionary development, the levels that self-creation should be based on.

Following this holistic paradigm, you will be able to *achieve personal self-realization and spiritual self-salvation.* Even though electronic intelligence is ruling the world, it should not rule us. Every one of us needs to retain his / her uniqueness and exceptionality and develop themselves into noble and spiritualized human beings with a new vision of the reality, able to create his / her inner perceptive device – *the auto-media of self-creation* that will help establish the unity of the conscious and subconscious minds. and make us more spiritually mature.

Thus, we'll be developing new life fractals of holistically-developed beings.

As science starts realizing, on the path of spiritual development, too, we need to perform *self-attunement to the Universal Intelligence - God.* Developing our conscious mind in synch with the sub-conscious one, we are developing super-consciousness, or super-*perception* that is making it possible to tune the mind and heart to the Super Mind that is governing all life in the Universe.

The Super-Mind releases the information that we tap into, and we need to learn to decipher it. When I write about auto-media, I mean our perceptive ability of the future that some most advanced minds already have. They tune to the higher vibrations and connect to them, being literally enlightened by them.

These vibrations are our navigating insights!

The Super-conscious mind works with us on the sub-conscious level all through the day, but to be able to tune to its massages and reason them out, we need to become *more conscious, more spiritually-intelligent, and much more realistically- perceptive of the information* that is being transmitted to us from the Above. That's another reason why our conscious living in the Now is so important.

In sum, every one of us is forming a life fractal, topped by **SELF-CONSCIOUSNESS** - *the highest level of self-awareness, self-reflection, and spiritual maturity.* but only the most intelligent, conscious, and soul-refined of us have developed it so far. Such intellectually spiritualized people are being helped by the Universal Consciousness and merge with it in the outcome.

The necessity to develop oneself is, in fact, *the process of developing such self-consciousness - the goal of our life on Earth.* Its development in human beings has been vital for the humanity for millennia. It is at the fore front of a personal growth now.

The Grid of Self-Consciousness to be evolved:

Super Level	Universal Consciousness	Universal Dimension
Macro Level	Super-Conscious Mind	Spiritual Dimension
Mezzo Level	Conscious Mind	Mental Dimension
Meta level	Sub-Conscious Mind	Emotional Dimension
Micro Level	Unconscious Mind	Physical Dimension

So, an advanced person who consciously steps on the path of personality formation is *self-generating* himself *(Synthesis)*. Then he is processing his life though self-enrichment, self-adjustment, or *self-installation* *(the stage of analysis)*. Finally, he completes his life by *self-realizing himself* and obtaining *self-salvation* which is the unification with the Source of Creation - God.

The holistic formula *synthesis-analysis-synthesis* *(S. Gazarkh, "Life at Large")* of the cycles of life that will be explored more below, is governing us on the path of self-installation in life, making it evident that without self-realization, there is no self-salvation.

Be sure to follow the he entire route in every dimension-physical, emotional, mental, spiritual, and universal. (See Book Rationale above)

Be Soul-Refining! Internalize and Externalize Your Becoming!

3. New, Holistic "We – Concept"

The new life fractals that we are forming now with the help of technology are being based on digitally-expanded intelligence that shapes our *new holistic self-concept,* the concept of the people that are blazing the trail of the computer science and are changing the world in an exponential way.

"Our seeing requires a correction of mind; just as clear vision requires a correction of the eyes. "(Alan W. Watts)

Changing ourselves and contributing our best to the world, we generate a new, holistic **We-Concept,** as the concept of social unification and mutual responsibility for the life on Earth. Our new digitally generated social connectedness is gradually forming our new society consciousness and the world consciousness at large.

The Grid of Consciousness Integration

Super Level	*Consciousness of God!*	**Universal Dimension**
Macro Level	*Consciousness of the Universe*	**Spiritual Dimension**
Mezzo Level	*Consciousness of the World*	**Mental Dimension**
Meta level	*Consciousness of the Society*	**Emotional Dimension**
Micro Level	*Consciousness of a Man*	**Physical Dimension**

The We-Concept, or consciousness of the society and the world, presented above is being formed by an unprecedented socialization and globalization of our lives and minds and our gradual self-consciousness ascending. We are, in fact developing *the holistic consciousness of inter-dependency*.

Be a Luminary to yourself and other people's cells!

The new We-Concept is also emerging in us as the result of our growing digital ingenuity and new perceptive sensitivity toward the information that is being transmitted to us from the Above. Again,

"As it is Above, so it is below!"

The information that is coming from the Universal Informational Field, an integral part of which" *the sphere of human thought* "is *(See Noo-Sphere by V. I. Vernadsky)* is enriching us with new self-knowledge, on the one hand, and holistic knowledge of life, or new Living Intelligence, on the other.

Let's change our Thinking Time into the Thinking Life!

4. Re-Invention of Self

A dynamic interplay of human consciousness that is changing rapidly with the technological evolution, demands every one's *re-invention of Self,* or CONQUERING of SELF in five levels: physical, emotional, mental, spiritual, and universal holistically. The three books on personality geology are based on these levels.

It means that we should ***put our minds and hearts in synch to obtain the symmetry of life*** that, according to *Dr. Steven Weinberg,* the Noble Prize winner, ***"is underlying everything."***

Intellectualize your heart and emotionalize the mind! Become one of a kind!

More particularly, the holistic philosophy of self-development that I am outlining here is meant to back you up in your self-installation by way of ***enhancing the growth of your self-consciousness*** in a beautiful symmetry with the Universal mind. The individualized vision of life comes with full awareness of what life is all about. We all have the gift of kindness and compassion at the bottom of our hearts, but we need to move these qualities to the forefront of our minds to be able to use them to our mutual advantage, de facto not just de juror.

We must ***synthesize the form and the content of the inner and outer life*** in accord with the present moment first to get more aware of life in general. Next, we need ***to analyze the life*** we live by becoming more rational and consciousness- driven. Finally, we will establish connection with to the Universal Intelligence, make individualized conscious decisions and accomplish the right outcome in life, getting to *the final synthesis* of our well-lived or wasted lives.

Synthesis - Analysis - Synthesis

(Internalizing the knowledge of life - **personalizing it** in the process of self-creation, and **externalizing it,** completing the assigned from the Above mission)

This holistic formula of life should be studied, reasoned out, and become the second nature with every human being on Earth. Each life must be ***self-individualized*** and cultivated by a person physically, ***emotionally, mentally, spiritually, and universally***, and the know-how of such education needs to be provided. (*See the Introduction*).

The stability of the internal world is the what gives us the God's reward!

"No Seed Grows Without Support." *(Proverbs 19, 6)*

5. The Holistic Life Paradigm!

To be able to meet the present-day intellectual challenges and to stabilize our emotional make-up, each person must work out his own *unique know-how* of synchronizing *the what* he does in life with the *how* of doing it. To put it differently, we need to put in synch the form and content of our lives.

Form + Content of our human essence in twine is a New Life Paradigm!

The Fractals of Spiritualized Beings:

Form + *Content*

(Body+ Spirit+ Mind) + (Self-Consciousness + Universal Consciousness)

Living Intelligence + *Enlightened Self-Consciousness = A Whole Self!*

To connect the form and content of our new, technologically-charged life paradigm, the society needs to give a chance to each living soul to improve the quality of his / her life knowingly and consciously. because the society's good depends on the good of each member of the society. It means that to become happy or, at least; life-content, we need to start putting our destabilized lives together and beautify our thoughts, looks, words, feelings and actions. As a great Russian writer Anton Chekov says, **"In a human being, everything must be beautiful: the face, the clothes, the words, and the thoughts."**

A great artist and philosopher, Nicolai Roerich put it differently. He said, **Beauty will save the world!** "Both most noble people meant that the beauty of a human being should be going in synch with the beauty of the world, based on universal beauty of the Golden Section's infinity. **Beauty is the inner world + the outer world's symmetry.** Naturally, our young people should be building their minds on the well sorted-out information, the knowledge that is loaded with *full awareness of the true, not virtual reality of life* and its incredible beauty that they need to be a part of. New Age philosophers promise us a great evolution of human beings in the anticipated Golden Age, but why not start generating these changes now?

To affect permanent mastery over our lives in a holistic way, we must change the nature of our thoughts and behaviors, that is, we absolutely must acquire the culture of holistic thinking, the culture of a whole human being, the person in whom **the body, spirit, mind, and soul** are in one inseparable unity.

"When we have Wholeness, we are Holy!" *(Deepak Chopra)*

6. "Ignorance is the Worst Enemy of the Humanity!"

Regrettably, the avalanche of ignorance in the thinking and behavior of many young people is appalling at present, and the darkness of their dogmatically-unconscious actions, often driven by the mass media indoctrination, is threatening the Universe.

Since we are not an isolated entity in the universe, and, therefore, an integral part of all that exists, our ignorant behavior and thoughtless actions affect the immediate social environment: our families, schools, jobs, and, ourselves.

We get constantly polluted and, therefore, disconnected with the Universal Intelligence that is governing our life digitally. Thus, we get negatively affected by the ***distorted form + content*** of our lives. We become toxic for ourselves and the people around us, and ***toxicity*** has become a psychological phenomenon. (*Psychology, May, June 2017*) Unfortunately, it *is* spreading among us and polluting our bodies, minds, and lives.

As a result, our minds and hearts, or our souls are getting more and more disconnected, too. With the holistic culture of living, we will learn to respect ***our Oneness***, irrespective of religion, skin color, values, traditions, and a social or financial status.

In the Orbit of the Sun, we are all , but One!

Consequently, we need to stop the distortion of the information that is transmitted to us from the Above. If we tune to it with awareness though our own auto-media and then structure our actions accordingly, our lives will get in order, and we will feel more content, happier, loved and loving.

The form (*our physical and material ways of life*) and ***the content of life*** (*how we live it, or our emotional, mental, spiritual, and universal advancement*) will be holistically united if we learn to be guided by this information consciously.

The form and content of life (***What + How)*** in synch is what we must accomplish in our internal and external life's electro-magnetic circuit that is generated with the initial ***synthesis of life*** (*the birth*), its ***analysis*** (*our processing the life energy through the allotted life time in space*) and the final ***synthesis*** (*the return of the soul to its original source.*)

I am sure the sacred geometry of ***The Flower of Life"***- our Merkabah, is working by the same principle. *(Drundalo Melchizedek)*

Synthesis -Analysis-Synthesis!

7. The Paradigm of a Personality Formation

For sure, a personality type person is the one that has the holistic awareness of what life is and the one that is constantly renewing it science-wise.

Information is ammunition!

Such a person does not depend on anyone's opinion. He is always looking at a bigger picture and can see things *from the holistic perspective*. He is not limited by stereotyped or inflated professional thinking. He has his own!

"Autonomy of thinking is a Must!" (Reid Hoffman)

Personable people also have the heart and the mind in synch and thanks to this rare quality, they are exuding passion for making a difference in the world. We have zillions of examples of the gifted people like that, but I would like to single out one outstanding man - *Steve Jobs*, the most personable man of our time that among many good and bad qualities of his had the three exceptional abilities that I consider to be pivotal in a personality formation.

First, he had a *holistic vision of his goal*, second - *the ability to select* valuable information from the redundant one and do the necessary mind-construction, and, third, he could strategize *the plan of action.* These are the basic three qualities of *the holistically-developed mind* that is following the universal paradigm of creation and that the humanity needs now.

Synthesis ⟶ *Analysis* ⟶ *Synthesis*

Steve Jobs could revolutionize the entrepreneurial digital world because he had a holistic vision of his goal in the mind, an exceptional ability *to select* the most meaningful information, feelings, and actions and then *architecture, design and strategize* the selected mental and emotional ingredients of his goal into a clear-cut and most reasonable plan of action. He also had amazing *team-building skills,* pertaining to the selection of the members of the team and the subsequent mind-construction of the idea he was architecting.

Idea + selection + mind construction lead to perfection!

So, to change the form and the content of your life and structure *a new holistic self-image,* that will be channeling you in life as a beacon of light and wholeness, you should follow the holistic paradigm of your self-installation in life. setting the goal, selecting the ways of accomplishing it, and strategizing the steps that lead to success.

Generalizing – Analyzing – Strategizing!

8. Taming the Inner Chaos

The three holistic abilities, mentioned above, are the product of the right, systematizing brain that we need to develop on the new steps of the evolution. We are overwhelmed by the avalanche of the information flow now, and this situation generates people's mental turmoil, emotional discord, and actionable impotency. It is the result of the chaotic supremacy of information over our unconsciously lived lives.

Disciplined thinking is the core of a personality formation!

There are very many **left-brained people** that are good at analyzing and detailing, but who lack the ability to **systematize and generalize.** That's why we have a lot of managers, but very few leaders who can **"tame the chaos"** *(Rav. P. S.Berg)* in their heads and hearts and declare the power of the conscious mind over the sub-conscious one. Science has it that the conscious mind controls only **5 %** of the brain, while **95%** of it is being controlled by the sub-conscious mind. It controls our behaviors, records our actions, and stores our bad habits that, according to Albert Einstein, *"have a good tendency – either you kill them, or they kill you."*

So, to develop a personality means **to empower the sub-conscious mind** that has an enormous creative power and make it your true friend. It will inevitably happen once you manage to control your sub-conscious mind consciously.

To be holistically alive means to be unconsciously conscious!

The ability for **selection and organization** that I have described above, are the most important qualities of a creative mind, the mind that works in synch with its two main brains: the conscious and the sub-conscious minds. **The unity of both minds is the sign of a holistically-developed mind** that real doers of life, such as: Steve Jobs, Elon Mask, Reid Hoffman and many of advanced-thinking scientists that I quote in the book, have. Finally, a holistically-developed person has **a rare ability to predict how things would play out in the future.** Only such minds are oriented toward **spontaneity of thinking** which is an extraordinary ability helping to cut the Gordian knots in any problematic life situation.

We need more of such characterful people in life! According to *Dr. Bruce Lipton* such qualities can be developed because we are not predisposed by our hereditary DNA to be brainy or brainless, to be second-rate people or to be geniuses. We can develop such qualities if we change our perception of life from unconscious and pre-programmed to the fully conscious and de-programmed.

Perception Determines the Reception!

9. Death of Ignorance

Interestingly, the quality of our cells is also directly related to the righteousness of our behaviors and the change in the basic substance of life in us –*the soul light.*

"Our cells in their joint work generate our consciousness." (Edgar Cayce)

The best of us are radiating the soul light, irrespective of the skin color, sexual orientation, or a religious affiliation. The inner beauty of such a person illuminates everyone around, and his / her soul's light, or **luminosity** tells us that such a person has found his / her way from darkness to light, from fear to self-confidence, from self-pity to self-love, from dis-connection to a life-long unity with the Divine.

Dr. Frederick Bell, the author of a very science-enriching book" **Death of Ignorance**" writes that this basic soul light is both positive and negative, as everything else in the magnetically-charged world. He applies the terms fire and water to the masculine and feminine principles, respectfully. *"As evolution advances, feminine souls display more of the fiery masculine qualities, while masculine souls take on the ethereal beauty of the feminine."*

Put in this light, our growing physical intelligence makes us understand that ***it is pointless to verge a fight against gay movement.*** Gay people are prone to their self-development as anyone else, and their choice is the matter of their own soul light and their own soul evolution. The most important thing is the richness of a person's aware intelligence and the level of his / her growing ***self-consciousness***!

Let's deprogram our brains without vanity, from religiousness to spirituality!

Unfortunately, the forces of attitude, hate, judgment, insensibility, and, most of all, ignorance prevail on the lower levels of intelligence development in this world. Apparently, consciousness needs to be considerably heightened so a person could be good, not just appear to be good, and could respect, not just appear to be respectful.

"Ignorance is the worst enemy of the humanity." (Albert Einstein)

Any transformation is the result of the power of thought that should be guided towards a goal-oriented, conscious and meaningful self-installation in life. All we should do is to sparkle those that get on this path with ***a wish for self-enrichment, self-installation, and self-realization*** and equip them with the psychological tools to do it consciously and without any sexual, racial, or religious prejudices.

"Man is a Free Agent!" *(Delia Lama)*

10. Self-Emancipation is a Real Salvation!

Considering the holistic paradigm of life, presented above, the Biblical formula *"Know Thyself!"* takes a new, holistic meaning, too. We know this provision of God, but we are not fully aware of how to do it. This situation is being generated by the technological revolution that is the greatest challenge we are facing these days, on the one hand, and that increases our dependence on it, on the other. Fortunately, inner discontent and the search for a balance in life push us forward onto the path of the spiritual quest, anyway. However, **to be godly in a godless world** of progressive de-humanization becomes more and more challenging.

A personal and spiritual growth is both a mental and material process, analogous to the growth of **a physical body, mental body, and body-consciousness.** Luckily, our appetite for knowledge starts with our searching for God and getting better informed about our bodies, health, and our spiritual existence. We get to know more about how the body functions, what energies it, and what forces operate in the twilight realm of matter, into which science is now groping its way in the search for yet unexplainable essence of consciousness.

"The only way to discover the limits of the possible is to go beyond them into the impossible." (Arthur C. Clark.)

The first level of our spiritual development that I call **Physical intelligence** (*See Part Two, Ch 3) i*ncorporates our inner integrity, our family values, and moral stand points, instilled in us by our parents. It also questions the existence of a super power over our lives and the authenticity of our faith in it. With knowledge about the body, we acquire more awareness about the quality of our life, and we obtain physical and mental maturity that helps the most willful and personable of us resist the mechanical reaction to life problems. As Mr. Ouspensky writes,

"There are only two forces struggling in the world -

consciousness and mechanicalness"

Edgar Cayce in his very thought-provoking book " **No Soul Left Behind**" notes that we are all guided by the standards that are shaped by our intelligence and the cultural environment that shapes these values. He writes, *"Only constructive, well-formed intelligence may make for better physical and mental development. What we think, what we put into the mind to work upon, to feed upon, to abide by is what we become because we are what our cells are"*.

Don't let anyone Script Your Actions or Monitor Your Life for you; Be a Self-Guru!

Don't Be Life-Negligent; Be Life-Intelligent!

Embrace Your Life without any Inner Strife!

Part Two

(The main parts of the book start here)

The Matrix of Personality Formation

(The Plan of Action)

"Being a personality is a life – earned accomplishment; it's not a given!" (Leo Vygotsky)

Whatever You Are, You Create!

1. The Ladder of Self-Resurrection

Following the *hierarchic structure of consciousness ascending,* presented above, we'll pursue the matrix of a personality development stage by stage.

We are not moving through life; life is moving through us!

Naturally, our mission if life is to realize the gifts that we are granted from the Above and raise the level of our spiritual vibrations to be able to come closer to the Creator in our self-creation in the *physical (mini), emotional (meta). mental (mezzo). spiritual (macro)* and *universal (super)* levels. The integration of all the levels progresses consciously to wholeness. On the path of wholeness, we become whole - *body + spirit + mind + self-consciousness + super-consciousness!*

The Ladder of Self-Resurrection:

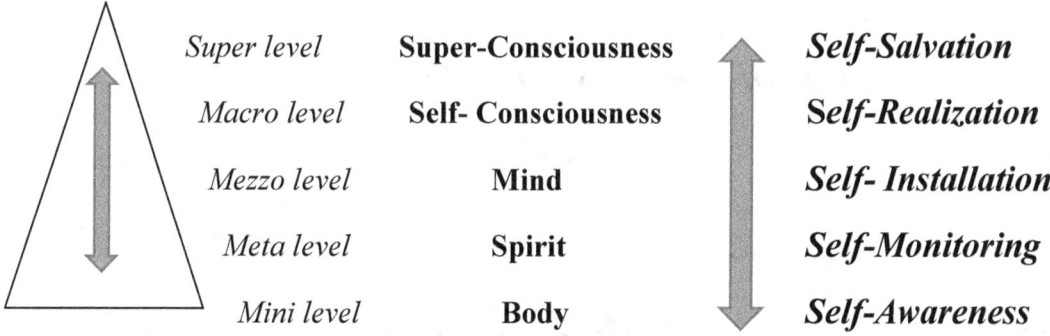

Super level	**Super-Consciousness**	*Self-Salvation*
Macro level	**Self-Consciousness**	*Self-Realization*
Mezzo level	**Mind**	*Self-Installation*
Meta level	**Spirit**	*Self-Monitoring*
Mini level	**Body**	*Self-Awareness*

Our happiness, therefore, *is* based on our fundamentally *conscious self-managing* that channels the mind, body, spirit, and consciousness toward holistic unity of self-created you. It starts with *self-knowledge* and *self-love* that are inseparable with the language, emotional, and moral *self-monitoring and self-refinement*. They, in turn, require constant intellectual self-sculpturing, self-adjustment, and *self-installation.* Processing oneself through all those stages consciously makes it possible for an individual to accomplish full professional and personal *self-realization* that culminates into a spiritual *self-salvation.*

Perceiving life consciously on this path will help you keep an eye on the brain, and it will discipline your thoughts, words, and emotions. Your ability for experimentation and inspiring yourself and the people around you will be amazing.

The energy field around you, or your *personal informational field* will be magnetized, not demagnetized, and it will exude the light of intelligence, charisma, and personal magnetism. You will proudly declare:

I Am the Whole Me; I am the Best I could Ever Be!

2. Personal Informational Electro-Magnetic Field

New science sees consciousness as the informational field of a person, connected to *the Universal Informational Field* that we are learning to tap now. As a matter of fact, every human being should develop the ability to charge his own personal informational field from the one that's everywhere around him and obtain *spiritual maturity* that will determine who he / she has become in life on the path of personality formation and *self-salvation.* Leo Vygotsky has a warning for us:

"Be concerned not with being a success, but with your life making sense!"

Developing yourself along the spheres if self-awareness and self-creation, designed below, you will enrich your intellectuality, obtain spiritual maturity and, most importantly, you will raise your **SELF-CONSCIOUSNESS** that, according to science, is of an electro-magnetic nature and that comprises your Personal Informational Field.

Life is an Evolving Spiral of Consciousness.

Universal	*Self-Salvation*	Dimension
Spiritual	*Self-Realization*	Dimension
Mental	*Self-Installation*	Dimension
Emotional	*Self-Monitoring*	Dimension
Physical	*Self-Awareness*	Dimension

The level of a person's informational field's vibration is always the same as the level of consciousness of the owner of the soul. The higher the level of the soul's vibration, the more refined the soul and its self-consciousness is, and so, it will go to a higher dimension at the outcome of a person's life.

Optimize the Soul's Size with the Self-Creation Device!

3. Step One - Upgrade Your Intelligence!

The first step on the path of becoming *the Whole, Superior You* is acquiring *Living Intelligence.* Behind our DNA is remarkable intelligence that is far too complex. Technological times need a much more advanced intelligence, *the intelligence of a holistic value*, embracing the five dimensions of life - *physical, emotional, mental, spiritual, and universal*, and incorporating the ten basic intelligences. *(See the chart below)* Evolutionary-advanced self-development appears to be the domain of higher consciousness and its biological nature in us. It is essential, therefore, to raise our consciousness by acquiring more living intelligence. *(See the Introduction)* Developing technologically-enriched intelligence is step one on this path. So, the book, featuring the mental level of the personality development geology, called *"Living Intelligence or the Art of Becoming!"* is focused on the ways to expand your intelligence. As Will Durant brilliantly put it, *"Education is a progressive discovery of your own ignorance."*

I suggest doing it holistically, by expanding your general and professional outlook in ten basic intelligences and five dimensions: *mini, meta, mezzo, macro, super*. The Art of Becoming is, in fact, *the blueprint of holistic self-creation* and the ladder of the mastery of intellectual faculties on the way to spiritual self-resurrection in life. With these intelligences, being developed in the holistic unity, we'll start emanating light from inside. *True Intelligence always shines!*

Vistas of Intelligence to Mount:

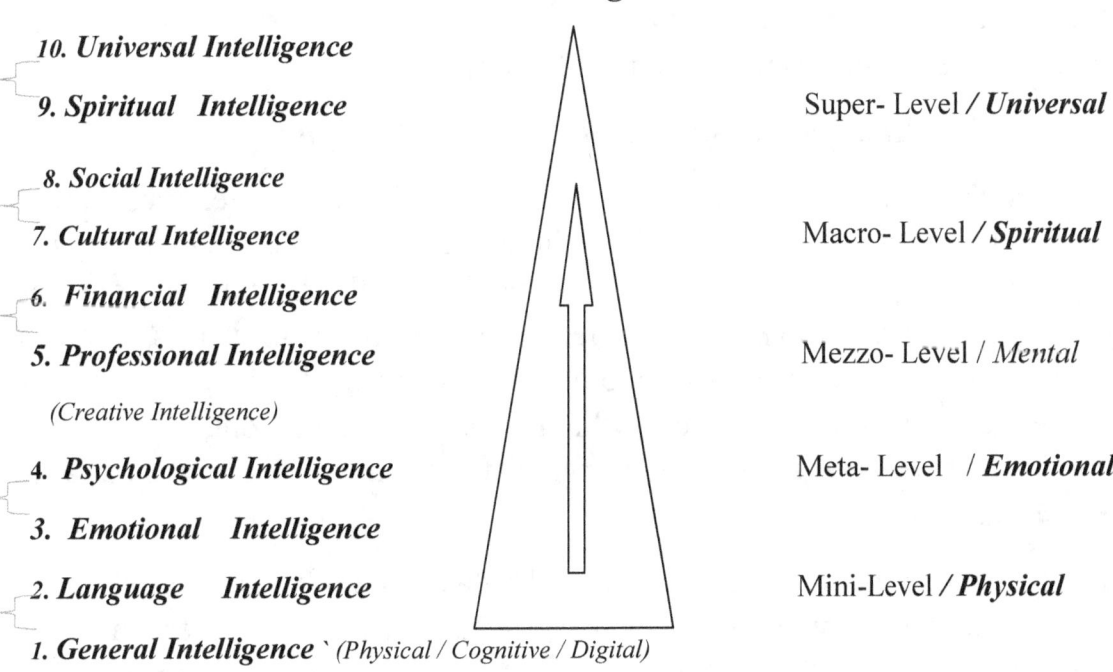

10. Universal Intelligence

9. Spiritual   Intelligence   Super- Level / *Universal*

8. Social Intelligence

7. Cultural Intelligence   Macro- Level / *Spiritual*

6. Financial   Intelligence

5. Professional Intelligence   Mezzo- Level / *Mental*

   (Creative Intelligence)

4. Psychological Intelligence   Meta- Level / *Emotional*

3. Emotional   Intelligence

2. Language   Intelligence   Mini-Level / *Physical*

1. General Intelligence `(Physical / Cognitive / Digital)*

Life Needs to Be Studied and Self-Guarded!

4. Step Two - Refine Your Soul!

The next step on the path of self-installation is presented in the second book of the trilogy, called "*Soul Refining.*" It is focusing on the most important aspects of **soul-refining and self-consciousness ascending** at the time when "*we teach robots to laugh.*" *("Scientific American Mind, May-June, 2017)* It also addresses the urgent necessity for all of us to preserve our souls at the time of a strong technological gust that blows away the connections between our souls.

A soul is a phenomenon of the etherical energy world, the level of vibration of which is always the same as the level of consciousness of the owner of the soul. So, the higher the level of the soul's vibration, the more refined the soul and its consciousness is, and to a higher dimension it will go to after a person's death.

Our spiritual wealth is defined by death!

Consciousness is our highest commodity, and once we realize the necessity to reason out the reality consciously, we'll transcend the limitations of our surroundings, resurrect our souls, change the culture of our thinking, and become masters of our destiny. Living intelligence becomes consciousness in action, the consciousness that cultivates *a new*, **HOLISTIC CULTURE OF BEING!**

The holistic culture of thinking and living, or consciousness development, is the culture that transcends "*the collective unconscious*" attitude to life in us. When a person is driven by the society's common sense or the crowd's mentality, he / she acts "*like a robot on a remote control*" *(David. Eike)*, and he / she is living in an automatic trance of unconscious patterns of behavior.

Many people's consciousness is just sleeping.

Their souls are disconnected, their spirituality is in dormant state, even though they might be religious. Their decisions, judgements, attitudes, and patterns of behavior are prompted by the social mass media and the human environment. They lack **individualized approach to life**, free of any outer influences. We are all yarning for life contentment - for more money to satisfy our immediate needs, for more self-recognition, for everything that our souls long for, but to accomplish that, we need to resist ignorance that puts our consciousness out of its **form and content.**

Obviously, developing intelligence, you need to take care of your innermost core, the **soul,** imbuing it with a stronger spirit and consciously reasoned out spirituality. In fact, refining our souls, we start developing "**spiritualized intelligence**" and obtaining **spiritual maturity.** Essentially, this evolutionary process is based on our various religious paradigms, and it is being built up with our exponentially growing intelligence. No wonder the mental dimension is the basis for the spiritual and universal levels of consciousness. *(See the book" Soul-Refining"- the emotional level)*

Soul-Refining is Life-Defining!

Science sees ***consciousness is the highest form of creative information.*** Therefore, consciousness development, or the process of consciousness ascending must be forming **as a hierarchic structure,** holographically reflecting everything else in the universe. *(See the structure of consciousness in the chart below.)* Spirituality, in turn, is forming our consciousness and raising it to new dimensions with our every conscious thought, word, and action. It happens thanks to the **mutation of all the levels of consciousness.**

We can compare this structure to the Russian Dolls, when a lover level incorporates all the rest, integrating the lower levels of consciousness into to the highest, universal one. I make a modest attempt to present my version of the **exponential growth of consciousness** in a simple way. *(See Ch. 7 above)*

"Life is not a circle, it's a spiral!" (Dr. Fred Bell)

Super Level	*Consciousness of God!*	**Universal Dimension**
Macro Level	*Consciousness of the Universe*	**Spiritual Dimension**
Mezzo Level	*Consciousness of the World*	**Mental Dimension**
Meta level	*Consciousness of the Society*	**Emotional Dimension**
Micro Level	*Consciousness of a Man*	**Physical Dimension**

All we should do is to know ourselves better and to be better aware of life around us to get out of the way of the evolutionary impulse to make us into the Star people. Only then will we be able to liberate the potential spiritual energy in us and **become free human beings with developed self-consciousness.** Let's also bless every intellectualized-spiritually person who illuminates the world with his / her presence in it. Thanks to them, we are learning to control our self-gratification impulses, over-power the vices, and develop class, elegance, and stature. It means we are becoming more self-observing, self-monitoring, and self-actualizing.

We are learning to be consciously self-conscious!

If you Aspire to Reach God,
Raise Your Intelligence + Consciousness a Lot!

5. Step Three – Modify Your Personality!

This is the stage of *self-fulfillment, self-actualization, and self-realization* in life, and it is the goal of this book. The five-dimensional matrix of self-formation that is presented above is, in fact, **the MATRIX** of a person's self-consciousness growth. It as is an on-going interdependent evolutionary process of a personality creation, or *self-installation in life* that is the goal of every human being on earth. According to Leo Vygotsky,

"You do not have a personality unless you develop one in yourself!"

By means of an exponential intelligence enrichment, soul refining, consciousness raising, intuition development, and ***constant inner-scanning,*** you can shape yourself into a magnetic personality that people gravitate to., You will become overly proud of yourself to rightfully declare,

"In my life quest, I am the best!"

As science has it, the Universal Mind first forms the **plan of ideas** and then materialize it into **the plan of reality**. We should do the same. We need to construct the plan of self-installation in life and then materialize it into a happy outcome of a purposefully-lived life

The five steps of self-consciousness ascending, presented above, integrates *physical, emotional, mental, spiritual, and universal* dimensions of life. Obviously, ***you need to maximize your intelligence and soul-refining on this path.*** I am sure you have heard people complaining that they visit the church every Sunday they pray regularly, but God rarely responds to their prayers. It is only natural because to tune to the Universal Mind that we call God, we need "to talk to Him" in the language of *spiritualized intelligence*, not just emotional outbursts, complaints, requests, and dogmatic believes.

In other words, you need to follow the *matrix of a personality formation* and mold yourself according to that matrix, without playing different roles in life and staging different games. Only authenticity generates intuition becomes the line of connection, your **AUTO-MEDIA** of communication with God. As a matter of fact, we live in two realities – our inner thinking world and the outer world of the environment. Since the outer world affects our lives more substantially, we feel discouraged and weak to resist its pressure and often redirect our lives in the way that suits us better because it does not require any effort to be applied. A great Buddhist mantra comes to mind here:

"Go Beyond, Fully Beyond, Completely Beyond!"

6. Perform Self-Sculpturing Without Fracturing!

Your inner world is comprised of the conscious and subconscious minds that in synch become a powerful tool of self-creation. When you put these forces together, as I describe in the next parts of the book, you will imbue yourself with *a strong spirit* that will make you practically unbeatable and your self-installation sure. Therefore, the spirit comes after the body in the holistic paradigm of self-creation, and that is why you are auto-suggestively inducted on each page

Body + spirit+ mind+ self-consciousness + super-consciousness.

In fact, according to David Broom, one of the greatest physicists and contemporaries of Albert Einstein," ***The mind is the hologram that is reflecting the holistic structure of the Universe and the spirit is its sustainer.***"

The greatest energy remains to be the energy of the unbeatable thee!

So, whatever you do and wherever you go, your thoughts in lieu with your spirit build up your reality and form you by uniting our conscious mind with the sub-conscious one, putting the conscious mind in charge of your speaking and acting. According to our outstanding contemporary, Dr. Bruce Lipton,

"God is in our neurons."

He means that our traits of character or God-given talents are not set in stone in our DNA. ***They can be modified by a person who programs his cells for creation*** and, thus, generates new neural connections in the brain. A self-modified person will develop his /her SELF-CONSCIOUSNESS and will have every right to say,

I have a New Seeing; I am a spiritually-evolved being!

In other words, you need to follow *the matrix of your personality formation* and then mold yourself according to that matrix, uplifting yourself to a higher level of self-consciousness that, according to science, is the highest form of information that is creating reality. Finally, the path of self-development or shaping of the personality is rightfully called by all new age thinkers the path of enlightenment - **the GATEWAY TO YOURSELF** through reasoning ,self-assessing and meditating - *synthesis-analysis-synthesis.* Unfortunately, the way we live and our material success in life determine our consciousness at present, while it should be the other way around -

The Level of Our Consciousness should determine the Way We Live!

7. The Matrix of a Personality Formation

In sum, *the School of Life* that I am writing about in the Preface is, in fact, the school of spiritual maturation that goes through the following five stages of self-monitoring: *1)* ***self-love****, or self-knowledge, 2) **self-management**, or self-adjustment, 3) **self-installation**, or self-actualization, 4) **self-realization**, or self-fulfillment*, and *5)* ***self-salvation****, or attaining spiritualized intelligence of the soul*.

This is the matrix of a personality formation is also the spiral a self-resurrection because the goal of following it is obtaining spiritualized intelligence and raising self-consciousness or **obtaining SPIRITAUAL MATURITY** that will make it possible for us to communicate with the Universal Intelligence. through the electro-magnetic field that is embracing us and that we are learning to tap now.

Our spirituality is holographic in nature, too.

We reflect the spirituality of the universe according to our level of ***spiritual maturity*** that is the main prerogative of a personality development. The higher the level of your *"**intellectualized spirituality**"*, the more meaningful and rewarding your life becomes.

So, turn your self-destructive mechanism into a self-constructive optimism!

Once you have decided to work on your personality installation holistically and take five steps of self-resurrection, you have made the first step on this path. Admittedly, it's not easy to set yourself in motion in this direction, but there is no other way to fix a broken connection between **the form and content** of our common life paradigm on the path of developing ourselves into *"**the Star People**" of the future*. *(John Baines)*

Stages of Spiritual Maturation and Soul Refinement

Universal Connection	***Self-Salvation***	*Universal Dimension*
Spiritual Maturity	***Self-Realization***	*Spiritual Dimension*
Mental Awareness	***Self- Installation***	*Mental Dimension*
Emotional Control	***Self- Monitoring***	*Emotional Dimension*
Physical Fitness	***Self- Knowledge***	*Physical Dimension*

Shaping a holistic personality in yourself is like building **the Self-Pyramid of life.** Five stages of holistic self-growth, presented in the chart above, are like the road in a thousand miles that begins with the first step. I am sure you are willing to make it, or have already made it. Next comes **step two** - the process of *selection* of the qualities that your personally needs to guide yourself by, and finally, **step three** - you will **strategize your life** up to the top of self-installation. Thus, your life will stop being the evil circle of repeating the same mistakes and patterns of behavior. You will achieve balance and full accord with Self, moving up the spiral of self-creation. Once again,

"Life is a Spiral, not a Circle." (Dr. Fred Bell)

The present-day science is uncovering the code of *"**how we fit in this eternal pattern of life**"* that Duane Elgen calls *"**the torus of the Living Universe.**"* Dr. Elgen writes that *"we can see the pattern in the DNA, in the apple, in the orange, and the structure of a small atom,"* concluding, *"**The Universe is the torus growing factory.**"* All this knowledge is mesmerizing, and our goal as educators is to make our students get inspired by the immensity of life and have an insatiable desire to decipher its secret.

To conclude this philosophical part, I suggest promoting exponential intelligence enrichment and holistic way of thinking and self-sculpturing in a spiral way, and I hope that while reading this book and working on developing a strong personable core in yourself, you will be channeling your thoughts in the right direction *to raise your spiritualized self-consciousness.* The book by Richard Wetherill, *"Right is Might!"* is my favorite one, and I am happy to declare,

Right is my Might!

To start thinking and acting in the right direction is the greatest benefit that we can get from reading any book that massages our souls and makes us better people. This book is also one more answer to the seemingly unanswerable question: How can one reach *internal equilibrium,* without becoming a monk, or without meditating regularly?

ACTIVE MEDITATION IS THE WAY TO SELF-RE-CREATION!

It can happen if we focus on *obtaining personal freedom and accomplishing personality development*, following the numerous examples of the most meaningful lives in the history of the humanity. As a woman who has lived half of her life teaching students from all over the world to pursue their goals and fly in their minds to the seemingly impossible personal destinations, I must admit that we have a great generation of young people that would like to live through an unpleasant caterpillar state to get to that of a butterfly.

"I am Not a Teacher, I am an Awakener!" (Robert Frost)

(End of the Introductory Part of the book)

Part Three

(Mini Level - Physical Dimension of Holistic Self- Development)

Self-Awareness

"I am the Alpha and Omega, the First and the Last."
I am the Love that ever lasts!

Self- Induction:

To Life -Thrive, You Need to Self-Derive!

To be Not Destroyed by Self-Love,

Give the World the Best you Have!

1. I Know Who I Am!

I am unique in every stance,
I was born, but only once,
There wasn't, there isn't, there won't ever be
Anyone like Me!

"Begin every day with the celebration of Self!"
(Paul Pearsall)

Auto-Induction;
I am My Best Friend;
I am My Beginning and My End!

2. The Spiral of Self-Growth

As I have shown in **the holistic methodology of self-creation** that the concepts of order, rationalized living, and holistic thinking are central in self-formation. Itt needs to be channeled by a person in a conscious way with a clear–cut idea of how he / she is self-developing in time and space. This path is not for those people that are self-creation oriented to just become successful money-wise. It's for those who are driven by an urge for full self-realization that eventually brings the most satisfactory. material pay-off.

Life is not phases and passages; it's the spiral of self-creation!

The blueprint of intelligence that I present as Step One on the path of self-creation in Book One of the trilogy, "*Living Intelligence or the Art of Becoming!" (Introduction,1)*) requires that you structure and consciously discipline your intellectual development first. **Self-awareness is key**! It is very chaotic now because it is not based on the *awareness of the outcome of self-formation.* I hear young people talk about their goals in terms of education and their future careers, but very rarely, if at all, they talk about creating themselves personally.

The Art of Living is, in fact, the Art of Becoming!

It is noteworthy to mention that I am not trying in any way to refer here to the neurological theory of multiple intelligences by a well-known American psychologist *Howard Gardner*. I think that this knowledge is very helpful for young people to make their career choices. It can direct them to their preferences and help them avoid unnecessary frustration in the future, but it does not tell them that the brain is a systemic structure and therefore, **constructive intelligence has a systemic, holistic structure**, too. The mind of a self-refining person shouldn't be messed up with redundant information. The information that is meant to be processed needs to be sorted out and based on a person's true calling. Only then does knowledge have a *generalizing – selecting - strategizing* make-up.

"The choices we make dictate the live we live!"

So, as early possible, you need to mark out **the most essential ten steps of intellectual self-development** *(Part Two, Ch. 3)* to handle that information creatively. Tracing your intelligence through the basic five philosophical dimensions and enriching it in ten levels, you will eventually accomplish the state of inner bliss that's attainable only if you manage to fully realize your inner potential or **become a Whole You!**

We Get a System where there is the Structure!

3. Personality Development Ecology

I am sure you have met people who have a lot of *personal integrity* and strong inner *magnetism.* Such people have a lot of charisma, and we often call them accomplished, but, unfortunately, in many cases, their accomplishments are measured by their bank accounts and career positions. **They are not holistically-developed** because the spiritual side of their personalities is often missing, and so, the pyramid of their self-installation is incomplete. There is no "*spiritualized intelligence* "in them.

But there are others that radiate knowledge and have unshakable values but are not necessarily materially secure. Such people are always self-made. well-read, and are very personable. They illuminate the space around them, and they are real *luminaries,* irrespective of their skin color and religious standards. I am sure that when the society starts helping the people of integrity and honor, the real revolutionaries, we'll move forward on the ladder of consciousness evolution with a much greater speed. Such people inspire and energize us with their self-confidence and unshakable faith. They change the make-up of the history. Julius Cesar, for example, had the motto in life that is an excellent proof of a great **PERSONAL INTEGRITY**. He inspired himself with the self-induction:

"Become equal among the first and the first among the equal!"

Steve Jobs put it exceptionally, too.

"Don't be content with just being the best. Be the only!"

As we learn about the neural mechanism of intelligence, prospects for enhancing such *inner integrity* and *perso*na*l magnetism* that, according to science have the neurological and electro - magnetic nature, become incredibly important. Like the ability for true love, they are the core of our existence in a holistic way, impossible without a purified notion of love and a conscious decision to transform oneself into a man / woman of honor.

Our social environment is very polluted at every level of self-installation. That's why I call the outcome of self-creation - *self-salvation*. You need to be conscious of the toxicity of your immediate and distant environment and be immune to any sarcasm, criticism, pessimism, or any other poisonous" *ism."* You have your spiritual wings from birth. Just let them grow and start flying. We are all born to fly, not to crawl, but only a few of us are able to sculpture themselves for flying and defy the gravity of the common-sense stereotyped way of life.

Those that Defy – Fly! Those that Crawl – Die!

4. Resist the Philosophy of Immediate Gratification!

Evolution wants us to develop our consciousness holistically, or to cultivate ourselves in the ***physical, emotional, mental, spiritual, and universal dimensions,*** so we could be at much higher vibrational level, closer to the Universal Intelligence that we call God. Naturally, the level of our spiritual vibrations will be transforming during our growing in time and space. Such self-development requires a rigorous preservation of individuality and a conscious control over our thinking, speaking, feeling, and acting.

Cognate, ergo, sum! I think; therefore, I am! (Descartes)

Unfortunately, many people suffer from "**cerebral unemployment.**" *(Robert Stone)* They are driven by the three beasts in life - the karmic passions of the unity of **mind -heart-sex**, presented by the numbers **666**. *(Rev. P. S. Berg)* It means that their life is mastered by *ignorance, indifference, and lack of control over the sex drive.* Unfortunately, it is downright impossible to break this vicious circle unless you reverse it into **mind + heart+ sex,** presented by the sacred numbers **999,** symbolizing the empowering unity of *intelligence, love, and controlled sex-drive.* These are the motors of self-installation in life. Your chance for self-realization and completing the unique mission, assigned to you from the Above, cannot be completed unless **you know who you are** and love the person that you are creating. Your spirit needs to be strong and goal-oriented.

The greatest spirit remains to be the spirit of the unbeatable Thee!

Since life is based on the vibration of energy, or the fluctuations of ***idea+ matter interplay***, our life is supposed to be a set of endless ups and downs that we must take for granted and adjust to with a positive, well-balanced, scientifically-informed attitude, demonstrating a firm determination to accomplish the granted mission. The inductive formula that must be instilled for life is:

"WILL YOUR LIFE MORE!" *(Carl Yung)* THAT'S THE LAW!

Life is a bumpy road, all right, but it's worth every step on the way to live it to your full potential, however tough it might turn out to be. If you work on your mission consciously and willfully, you'll eventually feel a great satisfaction with what you have sculptured of yourself on the path of putting **the form and the content of your life in synch.** So, put a lot of emotional gas into the personal tank of self-love and self- realization, and you will become the manager of your life.

The Philosophy of Immediate Gratification is too Shallow for a Great Nation!

5. Inner Dignity and Self-Identity

We are born with a tremendous possibility of intelligence. Each person has his personal level of intelligence, and if that level is too low, conceptually and culturally, it is difficult to attain a higher level of consciousness, but it is not altogether impossible. It just needs to be holistically-expanded.

The inner dignity of the whole is the aristocratism of your soul!

To begin with, you need a **clear-cut self-awareness** and **an inspiring self-image.** Self-concept is the way you think of yourself; self-image is your vision of this thinking. The person with such qualities has **an extraverted mind, but introverted feelings** that in synch grant him a well-developed intuition and self-sufficiency. Both are the abilities of the people of the future, and they should be developed in our kids that seem to be much more connected to the Universal Informational Field.

So, it is essential to accomplish the necessary intellectual basis of **self-knowledge** that will help you develop a personality with much higher awareness. We absolutely need to get rid of **DON QUIXOTE'S BLINDNESS** and stop fighting with our own windmills - the self-created patterns of behavior.

You need to change the subjective vision of life in you and form an objective, holistic vision of yourself in life!

Self-concept or a clear-cut self-identity is the starting point on this way. Usually, people who seek higher intelligence and who are emotionally mature are identified as personalities. They have a much broader view of life and of themselves in it. They are very personable, kind, compassionate, and giving. Also, they are extremely disciplined, well-organized, very demanding to themselves and to the people working with them. They are doing all kinds of good deeds because they have superior criteria in life. No wonder we call such people *quality people*. Pastor D. Jakes, being one of them, gives us good advice:

"Identity is your ability to use who you are to where you find yourself!"

Personable people shine from inside, and they are great role-models for those who pursue a holistic growth of a personality. Their self-confidence is contagious!

Even when the sky is heavily overcast, the Sun hasn't disappeared in the cloud's mass! It's there, it's in the blue;

It's Everywhere, It's in You!

6. Insightful Self-Quest is Abreast!

Naturally, your constructing a holistic self-concept is an action in process. First, you need to perform *constant self-analysis*, consciously assessing yourself in five levels and deciding what level needs more of your aware attention. It is an *integral process* that requires a lot of aware attention on your part and conscious self-examining and self-sculpturing.

"The unexamined life is not worth living!" (Socrates)

Your self-assessment will be gradually transforming into solid *self-knowledge*, *self-respect,* and *self-love,* rooted in your soul and based on the life pyramid:

Universal Connection	*Self-Salvation*	*Super level*
Spiritual Maturity	*Self-Realization*	*Macro level*
Mental Awareness	*Self-Installation*	*Mezzo level*
Emotional Control	*Self-Monitoring*	*Meta level*
Physical Fitness	*Self-Awareness*	*Mini level*

Raising your self-consciousness on this ladder, you start with self-knowledge and constant intellectual enrichment, develop objective self-management and self-adjustment, and, finally, accomplish the aspired *self-realization* that culminates in self-salvation. A wonderful example of a holistically-lived life is **Steve Jobs.** He was a totally *self-realized person of a holistic type* who had processed himself through all the levels of a personality formation and was one of an exceptional kind, the business genius of our generation, and a real role–model for generations of young, electronically-minded people because he had exceptional unity of

PROFESSIONAL INTELLIGENCE + PERSONAL INTEGRITY.

He gave a go-ahead to the intelligence of many other people, and he created the framework of opportunities and risky alternatives for the exploration of the artificial mind's possibilities that seem to be endless. He is a true role model to follow because *he was inspired and inspiring!*

Energy flows where aware attention goes!

In sum, you are working on the **PERSONAL cycle of SYNTHESIS-ANALYSIS-SYNTHESIS** that starts with self-knowledge, goes through three stages of analysis and culminates in self-salvation, a new, enriched synthesis of a personality formation, its outcome.

I am Free to Be a Conscious Me!

7. Psychological Intelligence a Must!

The mini-level of personality-development is a personal level of *self-revelation,* too. Being holistically self-aware is impossible without solid *psychological intelligence.* To put it differently, you need self-knowledge, backed up by the *psychological awareness* of who you are. It is the knowledge of your psychological make-up, and it can be obtained in zillions of books on psychology, on the Internet, or by reading self-help books. Your objective work on self-revelation is the initial stage of *self-generalization*, *(the first synthesis in the holistic formula of life)* when you need to rely on your own educated self-judgement to rightfully declare,

I am not driven by any common-sense scum - I know who I am!

The holistic self-image that you need to form, following the information below, will help you generate your inner fort, called *self-awareness.* It is, in fact, **"The Best of Me!"** self-image, gradually getting instilled in your inner vision, your sub-conscious mind *(the stage of analysis in the holistic formula of life)*. Download it as the plan of action and never delete it! All that's required of you is simple activity, instead of passivity. *"Will your mind more!"*

If what you have read so far makes sense to you, continue your *self-sculpturing* together with me. I will not load you up with psychological information that the Internet is full of. I will just try to stimulate your mind with food for thought and provide you with the *self-suggestive tools,* helping you justify your exceptionality and feel much prouder of yourself in the outcome.

Psychologically backed up self-awareness helps break the vicious circle of our negative behavioral patterns, dictated to us by the society, by our ignorance in the subject, and our *reactive impulsiveness* because of which we often forget about the value of life and its shiny side that we might be shadowing for ourselves and others.

Next, *do not self-sabotage your self-installation in life*. Eradicate doubts in the bud once you get aware of them, and create the space in the brain for enthusiasm, self-love, and self-confidence.

"If it's to be, it's up to me!"

Apparently, you need to be more fit to take sides in the fight of intelligence against ignorance, good against evil, success against failure, love against hate. Be sure to inject the mind-set below into your sagging psyche:

I Never Whine; I Shine!

8. The Trajectory of Personality Formation

The holistic self-image that I have referred to above must become the main incentive of your personality formation. I have outlined the first two steps *(the initial synthesis and the analysis of its formation above).* Now. we've come to ***the final synthesis*** of its construction - your holistic *"**The Best of Me!**"* self-image that I want to help you form with the tools, presented in the next chapters.

What do you think about yourself? Have you ever thought about the way people see you and perceive you? I am sure that you have taken this book into your hands because ***you know that you are very special,*** but you have not yet arrived at the point when nothing can shake you in this opinion. This work has helped many of my students become charismatic, out-spoken, and personable. No one holds a good opinion of a man who has a low opinion of himself. The feelings of self-acceptance are not instilled in our emotional and mental make-up overnight.

To do the most ***objective self-discovery*** in five dimensions*: physical, emotional, mental, spiritual, and universal,* you must ***perform a thorough selection and organization*** of the good and bad qualities that you have.

The next two chapters present the designs of the two pyramids of constructive and destructive character traits, presented in five levels of spiritual growth. I recommend you design *"**The Best of Me!**"* and *"**The Worst of Me!**"* pyramids - the positive and negative holistic images of yourself, following the ones below.

Based on such selectively-holistic work, I suggest drawing ***the final pyramid,*** called *"**The Ultimate Result Vision of My Self- Creation!**", **the URV***. Place it on the wall for you to see as a visual back-up of self-creation. During your goal-oriented self-creation, cross out the weaknesses on the negative pyramid and add the positive traits of character that you manage to develop to your ultimate self-vision pyramid *- **the trajectory of your self- installation*** in life that follows the holistic paradigm. *(See Part One, Ch. 7.)*

Synthesis-Analysis -Synthesis!

Remember what Dr. Lipton whom I have quoted above *(See Rationale, Ch. 4)* says about the importance of deprogramming our cells - ***our mini-computers.*** Dr. Lipton claims that we are not predisposed to be a certain way by our genes. The way we program our cells determines who we will become because we are ***the co-creators of ourselves,*** not the genes of our DNA- the matrix of our cells.

Program Yourself to Self-Excel!

9. "The Best of Me!" Self-Image

To help you form the holistic *"The Best of Me!* self-image, take a look at the piramid of some major self-constructive personality traits, presented in five dimensions. A common tool for analysing character strengths is *self-X-raying* or psychological self-surgery. I hope this chart will help you identify which strengths you can link your personality to.. You might want to intergrate them into your final *holistic self-image later..* Use the empty spaces to make helpful notes that will serve you best to design the positive pyramid of your present self-image. Go from top to bottom.

Universal Dimension

HIGH SELF-CONSCIOUSNESS, an altruist, resisting, beauty-embracing, information-having self-transcendence, enjoying life, *intuitive, appreciative, giving, reliable, evil-sensitive, very spiritual, super-conscious, etc.*

Spiritual Dimension

Godly, spiritual, evil-fighter, conscientious, intuitive, compassionate, kind, fair, having intelligence, heart and mind in synch, controlling, etc. *respectful loving, caring, empathetic, humility, having cultural and social forgiving, selfless, subconscious-*

Mental Dimension

Intelligent, knowledgeable, interested, receptive to new ideas, cooperative, having good judgement, demonstrating *having originality of thinking, creative, assertive, with leadership skills, realistic, financial intelligence, conscious, etc.*

Emotional Dimension

Emotional stability, language-taming, communicative, sympathetic, sensitive, taming anger, indifference, controlling *positive, respectful, agreeable, reserved cooperative, friendly, helpful, responsive, sex drive, showing class, self-confident, etc.*

Physical Dimension

Good health habits, high self-esteem, modesty, honesty, reliability, zest, smiley shining with inner beauty, considerate *industriousness, perseverance, self-efficacy, having responsibility, exuding love, self-respect, self-restriction. etc.*

I Am the Whole Me; I am the best I could Ever be!

10. "The Worst of Me" Self-Image

Now, look at pyramid of *the self-destructive character traits* that you do not want to have on the path of implementing your personality growth. Draw the pyramid of your bad traits of character that you see in yourself objectively and would like to get rid of. It will be your *"The Worst of Me"* self-image, also presented in five dimensions. These character traits are an indication of *the poverty of the soul, unable to sustain spiritual growth* and they must be illuminated willfully and consistently. The banal statement, *"No one is perfect!"* is just a justification for a person's lack of character and will-power.

Universal Dimension

Ignorant spiritually, not an altruist, discontent with life and himself, *disconnected from the Source, very unhappy,*

Spiritual Dimension

Godless, cheating, dishonest, sinful, cultural and social conditioning, pattered behaviors, unkind, vindictive *no moral intelligence, contaminated by constant internal conflict, driven by his not consciensious, unable to love, etc.*

Mental Dimension

Poorly educated, hardly ever reading, no nobleness, inconsiderate, bossy, ahead, unconsciuous behaviors, *intellectually lazy, authoritative, no fairness, selfish, chasing money, unwilling to think ignorant, stubbon, limited, etc.*

Emotional Dimension

emotionally unstable, moody, grumpy, conflicting, anxious, doubtful, reactive, attitude, risky sexual behaviors, untamed mouth, etc. *impulsive, fearful, aggressive, abusive, often angry, prone to infidelity, displays disrespectful, indifferent, rarely smiles,*

Physical Dimension

Bad health habits, gluttony, low self-esteem, risky behaviors, smoking, substance abuse, poor diet, no perseverance, selfishness, bad moods, dominant, grumpy. dissatisfied, no financial intelligence, bad manners, vanity etc

---

"Bad habits have a good tendency-
Either you Kill them, or they Kill You!" *Albert Einstein)*

11. Characteristics of an Advanced Soul

Before you start figuring out how to design the ***Ultimate Result Vision*** of yourself the ***URV*** of your growing personality, let's look at someone almost perfect, a person who possesses the characteristics beyond conventional thinking. It will be easier for you to visualize and draw the pyramid of life that you would like to ascend and follow as ***the Plan of Action*** for yourself. I am sure you have met a person like that at least once in life. These people are called ***luminaries, or sages*** because they have *high self-consciousness* and illuminate our lives with their personalities and very unconventional wisdom. They, of course, are not perfect because even the Golden Section has an imperfection that is infinite.

"Beauty of the soul is an attainable goal!" (Nickolas Roerich)

1. They live in the bliss of what life Is! They are rational, conscious, life-aware.

2. They are wise; they are intellectually-spiritualized!

2. Their spirituality is real, and it is connected to the Universal Intelligence. It spreads to everyone and everything: nature, animals, every living being on earth.

3. Their perception of the world goes beyond the skin color and religious preferences.

4. Their love is their guide; it is in their genes.

5 They are not materialistic. They are self-content and self-sufficient.

6. Their eyes are shiny, their voice is soft, the character is gentle.

7. Their thinking is slow, but very precise. They do not impose it on anyone.

8 Their language is respectful, controlled, sincere, exact. They say what they mean, and they mean what they say!

9. They exude inner balance, tranquility, and emotional equilibrium.

10. They never lose their identity.

11. Their personality magnetizes with immense inner knowing!

12. They demonstrate true self-love - no ambition, no Ego!

Nothing is impossible for the one who wants to be personable!

Live with Greatness, not Bleakness!

12. The Conceptual Hierarchy of the URV

A dynamic, developing, holistic *"Ice Best of Me"* self-image that you are to start forming will be changing during your personal growth, during your life time self-creation.

According to the holistic paradigm, your self-image is supposed to go through **the stages of generalization, selection,** and **strategizing** in your personality growth process. Mind you, the stages of the personality growth that are presented as the matrix of the personality formation and the holistic paradigm of self-consciousness growth follow the systemic formula of life that this book is based on:

Synthesis-Analysis -Synthesis

The stage of forming a holistic self-image *"The Best of Me!"* (*the Physical dimension on the Matrix of Self-Formation*)) is the stage of generalization, or the ***initial synthesis*** - Part One of the book - "Self- Knowledge." It is going to be your working self-image, designed as the result of the comparison of the two self-images of you:" **The Best of Me**! and *"The Worst of Me!"* in five dimensions, presented above.

The selection stage that is also the stage of **analysis** will be surveyed in Parts Two and Three of the book (*the emotional and mental dimensions*) – "Self-Monitoring" and "Self-Installation" parts of the book.

The working self-image, while transforming through the time and space, will eventually mutate into the **Ultimate Result Vision** of yourself - ***the final synthesis*** (*the spiritual and universal dimensions* – "Self-Realization" and "Self-Salvation" parts of the book). The Matrix of Personality Formation presents them all holistically.

There is no system without the structure!

It might take years, or even the entire life to install the **Ultimate Result Vison** of yourself, *or the URV in* the mind! Every person ends up being someone, and everyone ends up with his / her self-image as the ultimate result of his /her life.

Who you have become is your life's outcome!

Other than that, the vision of the best of you that you will be forming during your life time is crucial in following the matrix of self-installation for your sub-conscious and conscious minds because your conscious mind's successful overpowering the sub-conscious mind and making it your best friend determines the level of self-consciousness that you will ultimately obtain. It will become the ultimate result of your life.

This working self-image should be internalized and fully accepted by you, guiding you exponentially toward the ultimate result vision of your life.

Self-acceptance is an absolute must!

Mind you, however, that your life-transforming "T*he Best of Me!* self- image should not be the replica of any successful person, or any role model you know. It should be your individual portrait without any bad habits, or patterns of behavior that tend to dim your inner light and ***demagnetize your heart+ mind circuit.***

Don't imitate anyone's trap, be in the yourself unique wrap!

Also, you must be overly aware of your character weaknesses and want to consciously delete them from the interface of the ultimate result of your life. Learn to form a conceptual hierarchy of the URV of yourself gradually, at any given moment with the help of your own objective in-put.

Instead of self-guilt, develop self-support, self-love, and self-reward!

During your goal-oriented self-creation and in *the process of your self-designin*g, cross out the weaknesses on the negative pyramid of your destructive traits of character and add the positive traits of character that you manage to acquire to your new pyramid of life that will become the Ultimate Result Vision of the best of you. Induct yourself with the mind-set below:

I don't compete and don't compare!

I am just the best here and there!

I Can be the Best I am!

I Want to be the Best I am!

I Will be the Best I am!

I Choreograph My Personal Self-Drive to Thrive!

13. The Basic Self-Induction for Self-Production!

Now, you have come to the point in this book, when I need to introduce the **basic auto-induction** that will become your self-help device in any situation, be it a romantic enrolment, a family problem, or a job misunderstanding. There are very many self-inductions in this book, and you, for sure, have singled out some most working one's for you. Great! I am glad you find them helpful.

The one I am introducing below has been mentioned as the basic one in the first book on personality formation" *Living Intelligence or the Art of Becoming*!" As a matter of fact, it I has been **the self-inducting tool** for all my students for years, and it is the one I rely on myself. It will be handy in any situation as *your* psychological back-up, or *a self-hypnosis helping hand* .e.

Instead of being reactive, become responsively pro-active!

It is very simple, but extremely effective because it is easily memorized and character-molding. It has helped hundreds of my students on the path of intelligence-formation, career building, and self-installation. It is also very effective to conduct the Suggestive Meditation that I describe below.

I know who I am!

I am a strong, calm, and determined owner of my firm will!

I can do   whatever you need;

I want to …;

And I will…!

I am becoming better and better, kinder and kinder…. with each breath, (each coming moment, day, months, year).

(You need to regulate your breathing. Breathe in while inducting the first part of each statement in this formula. Make a short pause, while instilling it into the mind. Breathe out, when inwardly saying the second part of the statement.)

To be never upset, change your mind-set!

Note it, please, that your self-inducting will be very rough, unstable, and not consistent at the beginning. It's quite normal. Like everything else in life, self-inducting needs practice and persistence.

We are All Just Human Clay!

14. Stabilize Yourself in Every Cell!

The future of humans does not look promising as it encompasses the accelerated development of artificial intelligence without love and spiritual content. A new generation is raised on abstract, virtual, unspecified information that they get quickly adjusted to and acculturated by. The situation is getting worth. and we cannot, but act. As a great British writer Somerset Maugham writes,

"The mills of god grind slowly, but they grind exceedingly small!"

So, our managing ourselves in holistic self-growing requires **aware attention** paid to life constantly. Mind-mating is possible only if we return to the only place of power - *the present moment.*

Dealing with the present emotional trauma then and there and out-powering the negative emotions with the help of *the aware attention paid to the situation* returns us to the reality and does not leave the residue of the past emotional memory that poisons the lives of the ones involved in the conflict. Reaction, being reserved, will keep your emotional pendulum in a neutral surf, and you won't damage your cells that are the citizens of your body. Induct yourself with:

I develop a new fashion – love, beauty, and compassion!

There are wonderful examples of *the schools of ethics* in history – the school of gentlemen and ladies in Great Britain and the school of nobility in pre-revolutionary Russia. They have instilled in their learner's gallantry, manners, ethics, norms of noble behavior and reserved responses to any life challenges. They had been instilled in people for centuries. We still feel their contribution to the world in rare testimonials of such behavior. The etiquette, morals, polite rituals and restricted talking must be studied inductively in our schools now!

I know who I am!

I Can…! I Want to…! And I Will…!

What can we teach our future generation if they watch the TV programs that promote yelling, fighting, cake-throwing, and pushing, disrespect, aggression, and other animal-like behavior patterns? Thank goodness, neuroscience is behind this aspect of *emotional intelligence, introduced by Daniel Goldman,* the psychologist that I bow to. However, the know-how of this most important intelligence is not worked out yet. So, a well- known quote below never loses its freshness: *"If you don't have something nice to say, don't say anything at all!"*

To Be Immune to Any Toxic Spell, Stabilize Yourself!

15. Develop Love Intelligence without Negligence!

On the path of self-installation, *the most vital intelligence of all is love intelligence.* It permeates all the other levels of intelligence that you need to embrace on the escalator of personality formation. *(Preface, Step One)* Love is our main motor in life and the pushing ahead device that charges our personal informational field with undefeatable energy from bottom to top.

Love energy is our Perpetua Mobile!

The philosophy of love came to earth with Jesus Christ, but it had not been absorbed by our *hearts+ minds*, yet. Love intelligence is the hardest intelligence to obtain of all, and we must get trained for it from the earliest age possible. It is never too early, or too late to learn to love.

"Every child begins the world again,"

And every parent needs to build the core of his / her love stem!

We all have a different ability to love, depending on the way we were brought up - with the values of beauty of true love, or without it. A growing soul needs a lot of **love** *food* that they are supposed to be getting from beautiful, love and kindness- instilling world tales, soul-massaging cartoons, values instilling books, classical music, and the parents' intelligent channeling of their fragile soils.

The seed of love must be planted into the mind first with true-love relationships that also need to be addressed and governed by love-imbuing psychologists that instill in young minds the Cause-Effect and Reap and Sow Laws of good / bad outcomes in love.

"All relationships end; the question is when and how!"

Regrettably, *people are love-lazy." (Paul Pearsall)* So, love laziness is the weakness that should be eradicated first on the path of self-formation. Neuroscience proves now that *love has a neurological basis,* and it is hardwired into the architecture of our brains. To be love, we need to think love!

A mindless person is loveless!

There are at least two neurological mechanisms involved in the experience of love. First, love promotes positive effect of passion, soul-tuning, and self-sacrifice for love; second, it disables negative evaluations and criticisms that very often break up relationships and stop self-installation ambitions.

Illogical Love is just a Random Affair to Spare!

16. Sex Without Love is a Bluff!

By heightening the spiritual level of our consciousness, we are learning to have more *wisdom in love.* The higher forces of light, the Super Intelligence, or the Universal Mind that we call God always helps us on the true love path.

This is, in fact, the mental energy of the space, or the love energy.

Since we are One with the Universal Information Field, *(See Introduction)* each of us needs *to tune his / her inner musical instrument, the soul, to the vibrations of love on the Earth.* Our planet is a living organism that orchestrates the sounds of love in our lives and monitors these sounds *to harmony, not cacophony.* Unfortunately, casual relationships, playing games with love, and disrespecting its sacredness result in people losing their ability to love. Consequently, the search for the soul-mate often becomes endless and pointless. There are numerous examples around us testifying to the fact that **LOVE IS A SKILL**, and like any good skill, it needs to be instilled permanently in our consciousness.

Harmonize your heart and mind to be one of a kind!

Every love that is generated from the Above, or the one that starts with the *spiritual, mental, and emotional mating first* and goes to *the physical one next*, has the highest vibrations that make us look more beautiful, act at our best, and enjoy love for a long time.

"Love is not who you live with; love is who you cannot live without!"

However, living together and confronting everyday routine of life diminish love vibrations, and love, if it is not properly and timely handled gradually dies. Interestingly, the relationships that start with the lower vibrations, generated just at the physical level die out much quicker, if not immediately, because there is *no mind over matter wisdom* in such quick fix. So, teach your mind to love.

Learn to sound higher, shine brighter, and love longer!

Besides being a huge area of self-education, love is also the greatest incentive for *self-perfection*. Any change in a relationship can be brought about by changing ourselves. So, cultivate love in yourself and others. Rationalizing your love relationship *by connecting your mind and heart* and developing the ability to love by intuiting the future of a relationship will charge you with *love magnetism* without which you cannot be personable, loving and loved in return.

The More Love You Radiate, the Better is Your Fate!

Love Creation is My Inner Illumination!

17. The Grid of Love Consciousness

Most importantly, don't forget that you are working on self-improvement to accomplish your main goal in life - *raising your self- consciousness*. We cannot measure spirituality and consciousness with a yard stick of material success as many people do. Its effect is reflected in your intelligence, actions, in your grace and class. You must constantly *re-adjust your sense of values and consult your inner most self* to decide which way to go to become more compassionate, kind, considerate, language-fit, spiritual, and loving. Work on overpowering your sub-conscious mind consciously and develop high **LOVE - CONSCIOUSNESS.**

The Grid of Love Self-Consciousness!

Super Level	Universal Love	**Universal Dimension**
Macro Level	Super-Conscious Love	**Spiritual Dimension**
Mezzo Level	Conscious Love	**Mental Dimension**
Meta level	Sub-Conscious love	**Emotional Dimension**
Micro Level	Unconscious Love	**Physical Dimension**

I know my self-worth; I am not a love moth!

Be constantly aware of *the toxicity of many people* that are not self-creation minded and try to avoid any communication with those of your friends, colleagues, even your loved ones who might use their sarcasm to abuse, not to amuse, and whose attitude to love is dirty, disrespectful, casual, and cheap.

Keep privacy and regard your personal self-improvement in love relationship as *a highly private matter*. Give yourself a well-deserved self-boost and stay on the chosen path of growing love-consciousness religiously.

I know who I am!

I am a strong, calm, and determined owner of my firm will!

I can…; I want to …; And I will…!

I am raising my consciousness with each coming day!

You also need more *energy* and *motion*, or you need more *E-motion!* To attain more emotional energy every time that your spirit sags for whatever reason, you need to literally move and immediately fill your mental-emotional tank up with the *auto-suggestive gas of love.*

I Can Roam Any Terrain with Love in My Vein!

18. Be a Star! Love Yourself the Way You Are!

Since you are constantly sculpturing yourself and have every reason to be proud of yourself, **keep complementing yourself,** even if it seems to be an exaggeration. The brain will command the mind to change its self-image and refine your soul to the mold that you suggest to it.

Be in unity with your conscious and subconscious minds that will **work in synch under your conscious leadership.** All you need is to constantly absorb your individuality and singularity and magnetize yourself with more self-love.

Charge yourself with Personal Magnetism! It's your main "...izm!"

Do generalizing, selecting, and ***strategizing*** *(synthesis-analysis – synthesis)* of the steps that you take in dealing with any problem you face. When you develop the habit to do that, your life will stop getting on an automatic drive because your ***tactical steps*** in life will be always strategized for the most positive outcome. The auto-inductions, listed below, are good for complimenting yourself and backing up your ***"The Best of Me!"*** self-concept Do it while driving, walking, feeling bad, or meditating.

Induct yourself, breathing in the first part of the induction and breathing out the second one.

*1. I'm (state a younger age here) **years young!***

2. I'm healthy, good-looking, well-mannered!

3. I'm kind, nice, and amenable!

4. I'm patient, tolerant., and reliable!

6. I'm independent, self-reliant, and self-sufficient!

7. I'm hard-working, competent, and efficient!

8. I am determined, decisive, and aspiring!

9. I am loved, loving, and self-refining! etc.

Also, since charging yourself with ***personal magnetism*** and ***unbreakable integrity*** needs a lot of individualization of your attitude to yourself and the people around you, you might also want to stop comparing yourself to whoever and measure your inner transformation oy by your own self-image.

To Become Personable,

Make your Self-Creation Irreversible!

19. Protect Your Solar System!

Finishing my inducting you with self-knowledge, I would like to introduce *Auto-Suggestive Meditation of self-love* as active self-hypnosis that works excellently both with kids and grown-ups. It helps me and my students a lot at any time and in any place. You do not want to quieten your mind and get into the state of non-thinking. You just need to **actively program your mind consciously** against any negative energies and toxic influences that might affect you.

Your solar plexus is **the center of your solar system**. Put your hand there when you get into any negative field that might de-magnetize yours. Remember, everything has its own rhythm: digestion, blood pressure, pulse rate and body temperature. You are the one in charge of the fluctuations in your solar system. Your cells will follow your orchestration! Be a great conductor for them! Use this self-induction to boost your self-love and self-liking which, no doubt, will be mounting in you. **Give a boost to your spirit!**

1. Cross your arms as if hugging yourself on the shoulders so that the centers of your palms on both hands that represent the *solar plexus* of your body could be lying on the *edges of your shoulders*, on their rounding parts. *These are the spots of self-love!*

2. Now, embrace yourself in thus fashion most lovingly. Then, start moving your hands slowly down your arms, saying to yourself the following booster:

Auto-suggestion: ***I love myself the way I am!***

3. When your hands come to the point where **both palms meet**, make a short pause and say inwardly to yourself.

Auto-suggestion: ***If any one doesn't like me,*** *(breathe in)*

4. ***Next, shake off your hands vigorously***, thus removing any negative thoughts or feelings that you might have harbored against yourself or other people that may be having grudges against you and say:

Auto-suggestion: ***It's his or her problem, not Mine!*** *(breathe out)*

I know who I am!

With the help of this simple inspirational *self-hypnosis*, you can help your loved-ones, kids, anyone sculpture their sagging self-image, teaching them to do the same or changing the pronoun into "you." Your / their spirit will be backed up by **ACTIONABLE SELF-LOVE** and governed by aware, not pseudo-attention to life ,living, and self-refining.

I Never Lose the Sight of My Divine Might!

20. My Body is My Temple!

My body is my temple,
My mind is my priest,
My prayers are all mental
My faith will never seize!

"Have the faith in the seed that you plant to rejoice at the harvest."
(Proverbs 23,24)

Self-Induction:
I am a Self-Guru;
I Can Accomplish Whatever I Want to!

21. For the Reader to Consider

The First Stage of Spiritual Maturation and Soul Refinement

In sum, having done a substantial self-scanning, raised your ***self-awareness, enriched your self-knowledge, and fortified your self-love and self-confidence,*** be sure to boost your spirit with the first accomplishment ***at the mini-level*** *(physical)* of your personality-formation and self-creation –

"Know Thyself!"

.Remember, all the levels are integrally connected inwardly and outwardly to help you sculpture yourself holistically.

The Route of Self-Resurrection:

Universal Connection	**Self-Salvation**	*Universal Dimension*
Spiritual Maturity	**Self-Realization**	*Spiritual Dimension*
Mental Awareness	**Self-Installation**	*Mental Dimension*
Emotional Control	**Self-Monitoring**	*Emotional Dimension*
Body Fitness	**Self-Knowledge**	*Physical Dimension*

Keep developing your most personable qualities in their integral unity with all the levels of your holistic self-creation.

Self-Induction:

I Admit - I Am Physically-Fit!

End of the Part Three - Physical Dimension

Part Four
(Meta Level - Emotional Dimension of Holistic Self-Development)

Self-Monitoring

"The unexamined life is not worth living!"

(Socrates)

"

Self-Reflection is the Best Soul Connection!

To Avoid the Life's Gutter, Make Yourself Tougher!

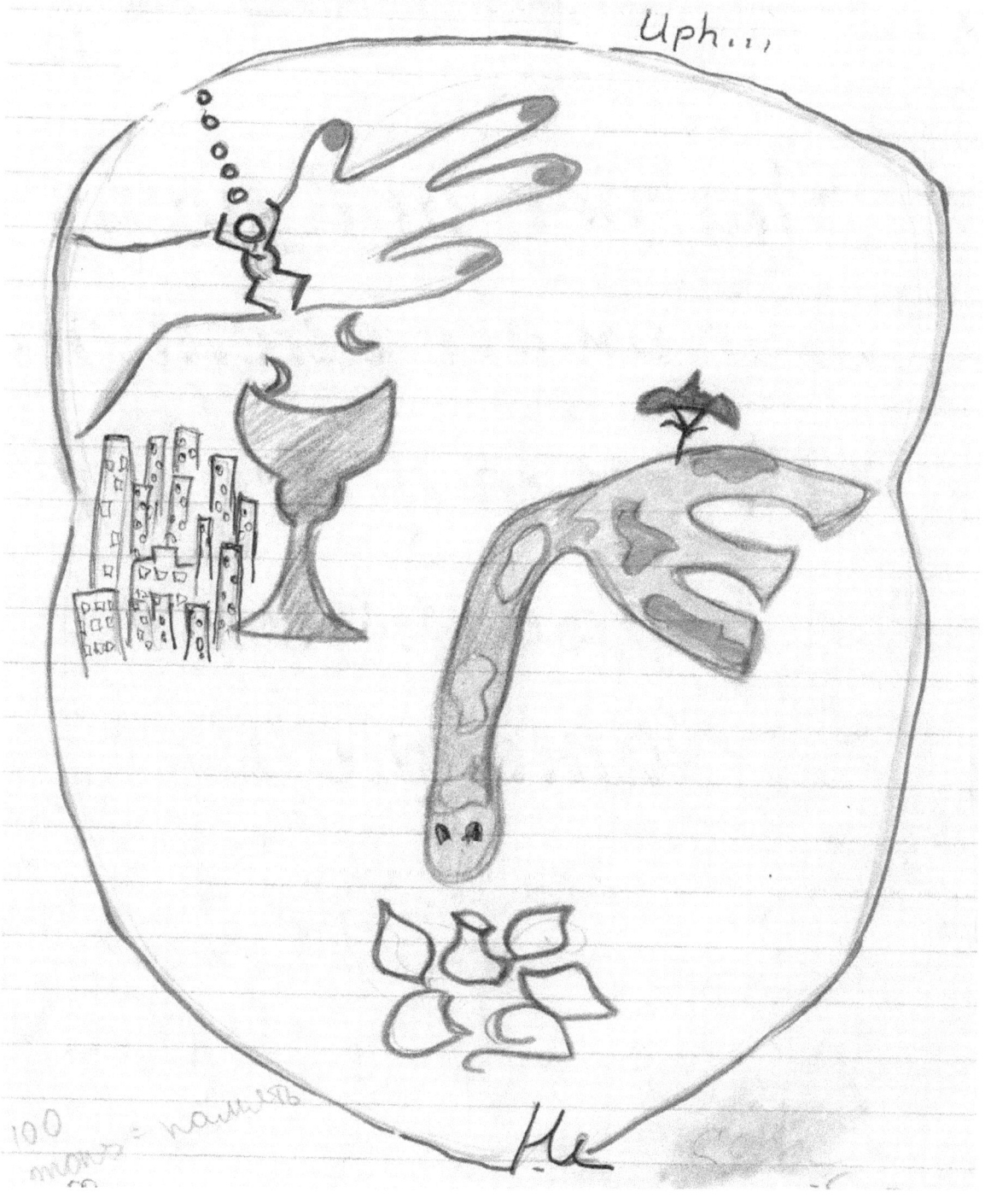

"To Be Free is to Stop Stumbling in the Dark of Your Soul." *(Osho)*

1. "A True Savant is Constructively Self-Conscious."
(Schopenhauer)

Sharpen and focus your aware attention To get to a Higher Consciousness dimension!

Self-Induction:

I do not depend on Anyone's Opinion;

I have My Own Personal Continuum!

2. Being the Best is a Tough Test!

(An Inspirational Booster)

Being the best
Is a tough test!

      But don't you fret it,
      Go for it and get it!

Whatever it might be,
Add to it some personal glee!

      Fear is, but the food
      That poisons your intentions and good mood!

It freezes your mind and body
And releases the self-pity zombie!

      To conquer the fear foe,
      Give it a striking blow!

Cut it in the bud,
And be done with that!

      Shakespeare was not wrong,
      "A light heart lives long!

So, harmonize your inner guts
And enjoy life in all its parts!

"Be Yourself! Your instincts always do you craft!"
(Queen Victoria)

"It's Not Enough to Be the Best; Be the Only!"

(Steve Jobs)

3. Self-Refinement is Mental First!

Your first step on the path of self-growth was taken. You have formed better ***self-awareness in five main dimensions***, and you have outlined the know-how for yourself to form a holistic self-image that is supposed to be a plan of action for quite some time. ***Self-knowledge should be consciously self-processed!*** I am sure you know from your own experience how difficult it is to stay focused and committed to anything. The words of Albert Einstein come to mind again:

"Bad habits have a good tendency- either you kill them, or they kill you".

The stage of self-monitoring or self-adjustment and self-management is an extremely challenging state because it is also ***the stage of emotional and mental maturation*** that we must go through when we are young, "entering big life". Bad habits that our sub-conscious mind had harbored keep pushing us back to the automatic reactions to life and its turmoil of changes. So, the main goal at this stage is **TO EMPOWER THE SUB-CONSCIOUS MIND CONSCIOUSLY!**

"Everything in the universe is mental. A human body is a mental energy conduit, too." (John Banes).

You need to learn ***to channel our mental energy in synch with the universal energy of creation that is mental***, too. Your ability to become the best of you in your self-realization in life and your happiness depend wholly on your ability to reason, to rationalize life, and to make conscious decisions. The world literature abounds in the examples of young, beautiful lives having been wasted because the young people with great goals and wonderful aspirations had no mental-emotional power to confront the challenges of life.

To preserve your personal form - "reject, resist, and reform!" *(Rev. P. S. Berg)*

Many people get destroyed in their holistic outfit due to the loss of goals, monetary difficulties, personal discontent, and the emotional turmoil. They are not aware of the subconscious mind driving their automatic actions and robotic behaviors that it had recorded during their previous lives. Self- creation is the way to battle this ***thinking inflation*** and start developing self-consciousness that is illuminating only intellectually-spiritualized souls!

The Fractals of Spiritualized Beings:

Form + *Content*

(Body+ Spirit+ Mind) + (Self-Consciousness + Universal Consciousness)

Living Intelligence + *Enlightened Self-Consciousness* = *A Whole Self!*

Unfortunately, people's mental and emotional hurdles make them helpless and unable to swim against the current of the common life stream. The snowballing of degradation begins, and it can only consciously and willfully be stopped. If that, God forbid, happens to you, get in charge of the mess in your head and start sorting it out because as the Russian proverb has it,

"Fish starts rotting from the head."

Freedom from *"the collective unconscious"* means freedom from the mental mess and emotional pain of futile suffering that unconscious living and robotized acting inflicted on us by the society's and people's imperfections. To differentiate oneself from the crowd mentality is the first step on the path of self-knowledge and self-love.

I know who I am!

I am a strong, calm, determined owner of my firm will!

I can…! I want to…1 and I will…!

We must consider that people execute their own spells on us by instilling in us their common-sense, society-programed perceptions, conditioned behavior patterns and emotional stereotypes of many dogmatically-religious norms, or street smarts - infested wisdom.

The present-day psychologists call the negative effect of people on each other – ***toxicity.*** Toxicity ruins our vibrations and messes up the personal information field that each of us is emitting. It de-magnetizes it and our will-power that is charging it. According to Reid Hoffman,

"Automation of thinking about oneself is a self-crime!"

In sum, to get on with your human evolution, you need to do a lot of self-monitoring and ***self-adjustment***! Only a rational and individual attitude to life can provide a qualitatively different inner content of it. Like the grass, finding its way to break through the concrete, you need to get rid of the society-conditioned outfit and become a free individual, able to think, talk, and act, or evolve, in ***a new embryo of spiritual life fractal.*** The World Informational Field that you are part of, has its own current for you. Tune your auto-media to its vibrations with the benefit for yourself, for many, for the world at large.

Form + content of your life will become the holographic matrix of the Universal Plan for you if you are strong and smart enough to get it.

Put the Strain on Your Sub-Conscious Brain!

4. A Free Man is a Self-Sufficient One!

A soul is a holographic entity, reflecting the universal structure of life. It gets in a frozen state after a person's death, and transforms back to life, reincarnates, when a person is born. If a growing person gets more and more ***spiritually-alive***, his soul is getting filled up with higher and higher level of consciousness. *(See Preface / Rationale, Ch 9)*

As is shown above, consciousness has a hierarchic structure and the holographic nature, and it is the essence of our lives. Living is, therefore, the process of adjusting, enriching, and refining our evolving consciousness, or ourselves.

Naturally, an insightful, rational, and aware perception of the world can be attained only by a well-developed, constantly self-improving, and an advanced-thinking human being. As Reid Hoffman puts it, *to run a successful start-up of you, you can and must think for yourself, create yourself, and invest in yourself!"*

Self-monitoring means constant self-reflection when your conscious mind takes charge of the sub-conscious one and helps you get in full accord with your creative ideas, emotional disturbances, and personal goals of self-realization.

You are on the self-installation path in an exponential way, not a linear one!

Now that you have formed the holistic self-image, you are living and monitoring yourself through the bad and good of life according to ***your own matrix of self-development!*** You are not addicted to things, to food, to anyone, or anything.

Practice detachment to any attachment!

Be attached only to the personality growth patch! You are not a burden for anyone; less of all to yourself! You are on the path of internal freedom, and you are always ready to induct yourself with the unshakable faith in yourself.

I am a strong, calm, and determined owner of my firm will!

I can…! I want to…1 and I will…!

Everyone has his own tempo of evolutionary growth. If your life is far from being good yet, don't get upset. Most importantly, you chose the best direction in it – ***the path of Self-Installation***!

Drive Consciously your Soul's Mobile;

Don't let it Stand Still!

5. Reflective Thinking and Self-Scanning

The evolution of our brain for 15 million years had to overcome innumerable obstacles, and we had to evolve overcoming them. Mastering your sub-conscious brain is a real challenge, but *you will have your own evolutionary leap without fail!* We all studied the Alphabet. Then we learnt to put letters together and form syllables. Later, we started making words, sentences and, finally, whole communicative utterances. Our brains have overcome many barriers, the most complicated one being *the barrier of ignorance.* Again,

"Ignorance is the greatest enemy of the humanity" (Albert Einstein)

Unfortunately, ignorance often puts us off the track, makes us helpless and irritable. and losing our stamina. Consequently, we sometimes say and do things that we might regret afterwards. But if you do your *self-scanning* and consult your conscience consciously to put the lost inner equilibrium back to normal, your sub-conscious mind will have to follow the conscious mind's lead eventually. Be sure to do the self-scanning in five levels to better place the problem of inner discontent.

The best power to attain is the power over yourself!

Next, I want to accentuate the idea of *conscience counselling* as the core of a continuous process of self-construction and self-consciousness raising. Conscience points out the imperfections that are still there and puts them to light It means that the pricks of conscience that bother you after you have done something bad, need your *aware attention, or* self- conscious and knowledge-fortified attention, be paid to the situation. This is when your *psychological-intelligence* (See. Part Two, Ch. 1) will be handy.

Be sure to pay aware attention to life without detention!

Aware attention must become your compass in self-creation. *It is the skill of the conscious mind*, and you should develop it at every level of your self-installation. The present day global international affairs, business communication, social and cultural contacts, and our virtual life are all based on the level of aware attention being paid to any problem in question. Regrettably, we have so much misunderstanding in all the areas of life because people are not well-informed. They operate with the *pseudo-attention, not aware attention, a*nd therefore, the problems start piling, instead of getting resolved.

So, Be More Self-Aware to Holistically-Beware!

6. Conscience Counselling

God is communicating with us through our conscience. Our conscience is the product of the subconscious mind, and it is connected to our intuition that is a direct line to the *Universal Informational Field* that the subconscious mind reflects in a holographic way. Like the AUTO-MEDIA that connects you to the Universal Mind on the mental level, conscience is your direct line to the emotional level .*Everything that you try to erase from the memory gets rooted in your conscience.* Conscience is also the cause-effect incentive for our prayers, meditation, and self-reflection. *Reflective thinking is inseparable with conscience.* It provides food for self-inductive work mentally and self-perfecting work emotionally *in the Now*, not retrospectively as we often tend to do.

"Thinking that is not rooted in the Now is dysfunctional." (Eckhart Tolle)

Living in the present is the quality trait that all of us need to work on tirelessly and consciously the entire life to be able to *defy the gravity of the common* and down to earth thinking and behavior. Be exceptional! You can do reflective thinking and actual re-unification with your *intuitive conscience - scanning* while walking, running, driving, while putting everything in order inside the house, the office, and inside yourself. So, learn to pay *aware attention to the pricks of conscience* and do conscious analysis of the reasons you have them in your soul.

Conscious and subconscious minds in twine are your tool for soul-refining!

In sum, every one of us needs to be constantly aware of the *mind and the heart* being in synch in any situation and at any given time. The disconnection of the heart and mind leads to failures and discords and to *the most painful twinges of conscience.* I talk about developing this **SACRED UNION** in the book "*Soul Refining,* "featuring the next , emotional level of self-growth. I keep reminding you about it because no work at self-construction is valid unless you have both the heart and the mind in **A LOVING DANCE OF EMOTIONAL DIPLOMACY.** By self-monitoring your inner mental-emotional climate and facing up to your mistakes and false interpretations of the reality, you delete them from your subconscious mind, providing space for new, carefully selected, and strategized actions. Congratulation, "*synthesis-analysis-synthesis*" paradigm is in action!

Put Your Actions and Conscience in synch;

Feel, but Think!

7. Self-Taming is the Main Personal Gaining!

Undoubtedly, we need to provide congenial conditions for a personality's growth because there are many things that are upsetting such growth at present, pushing our young people on the path of immediate gratification, robot-like living, money and fun chasing, and lack of moral intelligence. ***Our young generation has no self-monitoring skills!*** Therefore, they are lacking in mistake alertness and self-realization aspirations, let alone plans for self-formation and re-formation.

Working with young people from all over the world, I've come to realize that ***self-education and self-formation*** are not in fashion now because the society has no personality-developing tools. Young people are more career-oriented and fun life focused. Personal exceptionality is viewed as an unnecessary burden that needs to be shaken off the shoulders and erased from the mind, not to be labelled as a nerd or a freak.

Being cool is being a fool!

But, as social beings, we are not only teachers for others, ***we are teachers for ourselves*** first. In fact, ***we are self-psychologists,*** and we should be shaping our self-images auto-suggestively, not under the pressure of the commonly - adopted philosophy of life, or anyone's well-wishing.

There are two ways of teaching someone: ***direct knowledge*** and ***indirect knowledge***. Direct knowledge is delivered directly, perceived automatically, and stored unconsciously, and this is the way young people perceive the religious wisdom or anyone's soul-straightening advice. ***Indirect learning*** requires knowledge to be consciously processed, perceived, and reasoned out. This is how you need to channel your thinking in the attempt t***o tame your bad habits and patterns of behavior*** that, like pests, emerge on the screen of your self-consciousness and dim it.

According to the Law of Attraction, like attracts like, and therefore, negativity attracts negativity., generating a very toxic environment for your self-growth. Stepping on the path of self- installation in life, you need to be strong and immune to any toxicity. If you character and will-power are not strong enough ***"to reject, resist, and reform"*** the bad traits of character that you need to eradicate in yourself, you'll fall victim of the stereotyped mode of life again and again.

Be Immune to the Poison of Life!

Resist the Evil Stuff!

8. Don't Rust from Lust!

I keep repeating some quotes and self-induction because *"repetition is the Mother of learning,"* and some fundamental things need to be consciously digested by the mind before they get instilled in the sub-conscious mind. So, I would like to mention again Ravi P. S. Berg's most informative and wisdom-developing book *"Taming the Chaos"* that I have commented on twice above teaches us how to tame our untamable sex drive with the help of the mind. As a matter of fact, the battle between the good and the evil in us can be won only by *self-taming or* taming the chaos inside us.

The process of self-taming is a life-long process!

A great French writer - poet *Antoine de Saint Exupery* in his very inspiring and philosophical book, *"The Little Prince"* describes a lamplighter who wasted his life, blindly following orders and extinguishing and relighting a lamp once a minute. It's a great analogy to the people who *extinguish the inner light of their souls* and then try to relight it, hoping that one day it will become a lantern. It never happens because the lamplight will have no torch to do it. Therefore, lighting candles in the church on Sundays, but extinguishing light in the souls of other people is inexcusable and spiritually deadly.

The torch is the inspiration that is driving your personality-formation.

In sum, lighting the torch of self- installation in life needs structure as every other action that we take. It requires *generalization, selection, and strategizing* of every thought you have, every word you say, and every action you take.

Synthesis- analysis -synthesis!

Self-creation in five levels should also be a very *intimate* one, and it needs complete privacy. You cannot take orders from anyone or anyone's criticism to do it because it will blow off the torch of inspiration in you. You know better because you know who you are!

"A man of knowledge restrains his words." (Proverb 17,27)

However, these intentions of vigilant self-monitoring will remain just words, if you do not start changing yourself with better intelligence and self- awareness. *"Without knowing what we really are, we cannot refine even one cell in our bodies."* *(Don Miguel Ruiz)* Sculpturing yourself, you are charging the electro-magnetic field around you and raising your self-consciousness.

The Battle for a Personable Self is won by Yourself!

9. Love or Lust, Who Can I Trust?

(An Inspirational Booster)

I coax my daughter, as all moms do,

To end her endless love ado,

    "To turn love into a marital bliss"

    Love the one you are with!"

Mom, she retorts,

Breaking the train of my thoughts,

    "There is no love; it's only lust

    That takes the grips on us so fast!

When you are in the USA

It's a one-night stand that has its say!"

    Therefore, it's hard to tell today

    Which is love or lust, per say

The evils of a one-night stand

Ruin the love castle sand

    Love goes down the drain

    In our instant gratification brain!

The hopes and stomach butterflies

Have the life span of daily flies!

    Marriage lasts, but a little while

    It even stars with a sarcastic devil's smile!

It's the money force

That rules any love's worth!

Being loaded

Is what makes love molded!

Without a solid financial stand

You've got love with no refund!

The cancer of such love value

Spreads worldwide with the speed of the mildew

Is there any review on how to turn love mildew

Into pure love-lasting dew

That reflects the sunrise of passion

And the sunset of compassion,

That has much understanding

And is no mutual respect withstanding!

We need love that forms

Inspires and transforms!

But such love needs to be taught and learnt;

It must be reinstalled in our young generation's Fort!

And since it's in everyone's gene,

It should also be released on the social scene!

Love by the Moral Code;

Love is in Our Spiritual Mold!

10. Magnetization vs. Demagnetization

Life is channeled in us by the Universal Intelligence on the mental basis, and we must give it a careful thought in any situation. Our understanding of this fundamental statement helps us survive through the most emotionally strenuous situations in life. The first reactive impulse of anyone who was insulted is to lash back. But the proactive, mind-governed response is to restrict that impulse and instead of reacting, respond!

Christ's philosophy remains to be unbeatable!

It is much more beneficial for a person to take control of a negative emotion, or the urge to strike back verbally. One absolutely needs to out-power his emotions with the mind.

Intellectualize the heart and emotionalize the mind! Be one of a kind!

Our hearts and minds are now in defiance! We have de-magnetized them with our indifference and a "whatever "attitude to life. There are two types of people – **magnetized and de-magnetized, conscious** and **unconscious**, able to reason and unreasonable ones. The re-formation of our negative patterns into the positive ones demands our focusing unapologetically on the rule:

Monitor yourself! First think, then say, then do!

Self-regret and guilt demagnetize and victimize you. The cone of intelligence should be placed above the cone of emotions – **the mental level goes after the emotional one on the matrix of self-consciousness development**. This necessity is directly attributable to a personality development issues because the qualities of kindnesses and compassion are not just inherited, they should be raised in kids and trained by an adult person for the rest of his / her life. Our common goal in life is to log our biological computers to the Universal Electro-Magnetic Field through our perceptive antennas - our auto-media of life perception.

If your goal is authentic, you get magnetized from Above to realize it!

The Universal intelligence is always channeling us in the right direction. But this information is not given to everyone. The universally- governed *magnetization* always depends on a person's spiritual and intellectual make-up or on the level of a person's consciousness. Regrettably, *"most of the people on earth see the world through grey contact lenses." Tikhoplav V.U. and Tikhoplav T. S.)*

Stay in the Magnetic Store – Magnetize Your Core!

11. Spreading Love Magnetism

Allow me to remind you again that on the track of self-monitoring and self-management, *love is the greatest incentive for self-perfection.* You need to process all the character traits that you have selected for your self-image through the grid of love and see if you qualify to be a loving personality.

Love Skills are the top skills in personality formation!

You need to develop love skills in yourself consciously and continuously, as any other skill that I have outlined above.

The intelligence of love is the most synergistic one; it's the energy of creation!

Love's positive energy can overcome any obstacles, and it is *love intelligence that is at the core of mind + heart connection*. It is only natural because love is the sacred territory of the right hemisphere of the brain that harbors our creative abilities. There is a common view that opposites attract in love and therefore, psychological opposites live happier. This observation doesn't hold ground.

To begin with, you need to connect with the object of your affection *on the spiritual, mental, emotional, and physical levels* to lay the foundation for a long-lasting relationship. Start a relationship with finding a common ground in spirituality, intelligence, emotional attachments, and then, having been electrically charged on these levels of love connection, let it culminate into the physical contact. The relationship that starts from the Above, is God-guided and it gets solidified gradually, but surely. It will be amazingly rewarding, enriching, and inspirational for your personal and spiritual growth because your *love will be maturing consciously*. As a result, your will be rewarded with true, lasting, committed love.

Clicking with a person on higher levels illustrates the work of the cosmic **Law of Attraction.** Science has it that men are mostly negatively charged, while women are positively charged. That's only partially true because we have both charges as magnetic entities. The point is, which charge is stronger **to sustain love magnetization,** or a quick fix relationship de-magnetization.

Like attacks like!

The identical personal magnetism of love, based on spiritual values, intelligence and matured emotional affection will glue you together for years to come! So, the choices that we make in marriage are fundamental in life. The wisdom of all the sacred books teaches men *"to beware the charms of a stray woman"* and pay more attention to the way a woman talks, rather than looks, demonstrating her innermost beauty and intellect. Therefore, we often say, *"Beauty comes from within!"* The Russian wisdom says," *Choosing a wife, pay attention how the girl talks."* The Eastern wisdom has it,

"An empty jug gives a beautiful sound but cannot whet your thirst."

As far as the choice of the right man is concerned, I like another Russian saying:

"If a man is more handsome than a monkey, but is very intelligent,

he is the best match for you!

Obviously, intelligence of an object of love has been valued by humanity for centuries, to say nothing about the religious bonds and a sacred attachment to God.

The unity of the hearts and the minds binds!

Also, the ability to love is essential in life on a personality formation track because it helps to put both, **right and left brains in synch** and generate **the work of the one-pointed mind** – the mind of the man / woman of the highest intellectual capacity and personal integrity. No wonder the jewels of the mind and heart connection have enlightened the most famous scientists, writers, poets, musicians, etc.

Love enflames the heart, inspires the mind, and makes you one of a kind!

Most importantly, *love expands the bio-field of a person in love* and creates the atmosphere of synergy around him / her. Its trajectory is:

Mind - to - Mind	→	*Smile - to – Smile;*
Hug - to - Hug	→	*Heart–to -Heart;*
Eyes - to - Eyes	→	*Love - to – Love;*
Ears - to - Ears	→	*Soul - to – Soul!*

Sex without love is a self-destructive bluff!

Finally. love is our direct line to the Universal Intelligence, **the Omnipresent God.** When we love, we are immediately connected to the Above and guided by love. Most importantly, love heightens the level of the soul's vibrations and, therefore, its spirituality. Only true love has the constructive power for your self-installation in life! So, make love your identity!

Self-Induction:

Love is Me; Love is My Philosophy!

12. Emotional Self-Awareness

I have mentioned in Part Two the necessity to acquire *the psychological intelligence* to design the" *The Best of Me* "self-image at the first stage of self-creation. If self-awareness is the starting point in self-formation, *emotional awareness* is key at all the levels of self-creation, and it's the weakest one in us.

You should be aware of what activates your emotional key-board.

You need to have a clear-cut idea what keys you, not anyone, need to push to make you sound pianissimo or crescendo. The problem is, you *must be a self-playing instrument,* not an automatic piano that is coded for a certain melody by anyone: your loved one, kids, or any authority.

Emotional awareness means you are the pianist, not the piano!

Also, you need to develop the ability to use emotions to enhance thought; *you need auto-suggestive skills of monitoring yourself.* Learn to motivate yourself to reach any goal and maintain a positive attitude even when you experience most challenging difficulties. That is why the Auto-Suggestive Psychology is so beneficial for self-creation. You learn to be self-inspiring and self-supporting without expecting any emotional and psychological back-up from anyone.

Self- efficiency and self-sufficiency will become your self-prophecy!

It's a good idea to follow Edgar Cayce's suggestion of giving the mind the authoritative command *"Halt!"* whenever negative thoughts or emotions take the upper hand of you. Trace them down next to the cause and illuminate the consequences with your conscious reasoning.

To stop the undercurrent of emotional unease,

detect the cause of the dis-ease and illuminate the freeze!

Finally, learn to *plant the seeds of contentment and joy* for everything that is happening in your life. Be aware that the vibrations that you emanate get back to you in a magnified form from the Universal Electro-Magnetic Field. If you emit the negative thoughts and emotions, you will get them back in the form that is twice as strong and excruciating. But if you send love, kindness, compassion, care, and consideration, they will come back to you in a doubled form of some one's gratitude and appreciation. *Controlling your emotions consciously*, you can monitor the occurrences in your life better. and become much happier.

Don't be Emotionally Stuck; Create Luck!

13. Language – Speech Awareness

The spiritualized intelligence that you are working on cannot be obtained without *a tight language control*, either. Language awareness is essential for your self-installation inwardly and outwardly. Language is the basis of our intelligence. and *the most difficult one to monitor*. because it requires thorough shaping from berth. Attitude, grace, tact, looks, manners are generated in us by our parents and the environment. However, it's never too late to re-shape yourself, if need be.

Reserved, responsive speaking skills can be taught and must be learned!

Unfortunately, numerous TV shows demonstrate de-magnetized yelling, cursing, aggressiveness, and reactive tongue-lashing. Such language behavior becomes a habit that is very difficult to rid of. As a great Spanish linguist, Fernando Lazaro Career, most rightly noted,

"Language is the Skin of the Soul!"

In other words, language shapes our thoughts, words, attitudes, and habits. The self-inductive boosters in this book help you acquire *emotional diplomacy,* and they all contain the right messages. Other than that, they send the influx of energy into your conscious mind and wake you up to the innate right in your soul.

Language is also the passport of your personality!

Also, the way you word out your thoughts boosts yours will-power and the spirit. Both inwardly and outwardly, controlled language habits promote your *head + heart awakening* that imbues you with kindness and compassion, patience and understanding, tact and tolerance. The moment you open your mouth, the people place your intelligence, class, education, and character.

"The limits of your language are the limits of your world!"

Your casual speaking, texting, disrespectful treatment of the grammar of the language and its incredible lexical treasures indicate that you do not care what impression you make on people and how they place you by your language. Many young people communicate with just ten junk words in their vocabulary stock.

Don't humiliate yourself in the limited language cell.

Many people's casual speaking indicates lack of self-respect and dignity. They seem to be standing up for themselves in their language behavior, but, in fact, they just demonstrate ignorance and self-negligence and spit into their own souls.

Internalize Your Emotions, Externalize Your Mind!

14. Take Charge of Your Internal Pharmacy!

As mental creatures, we must oversee our merging with the Universal Energy Field at every level because we have the divine purpose to become One with the Universal Intelligence. So, your next concern on the ladder of consciousness should be *your body* and your intention to preserve it as the vessel of your immortal soul. The eternal philosophy of Jesus Christ is based on our consciousness ascending and heart-felt service to people. Internalize it without outward demonstration of your unshakable faith in public.

There are zillions of books on a healthy life style. However, bettering yourself holistically, you need *to work out your own set of instructions and prescriptions* for your body on all the levels. To put it differently, it's essential *to have your own physical, emotional, mental, and spiritual medication* in the form of the best-healing mind-sets to uplift your spirit and to heal any organ of your body and its cells with a healing touch and an inspiring word.

Know thyself at each level and in every dimension!

1. Physical Level - Health, exercises, nutrition, stress management, language rationality, speech immunity to foul language or negative talking, digital skills

All disease is brain disease! Keep an eye on your brain! Charge it positively!

2. Emotional Level - Controlling emotions and developing the feelings of love and synergy.

A smile, a posture, and a good mood are my emotional food!

3. Mental Level - A lot of quality reading, thinking, visualizing, rationalizing, planning, systematizing, studying, and positively projecting. Exercise your thinking!

Mind over matter is our common strata!

4. Spiritual Level – Honest service, creative work, interpersonal open, cultural enrichment and responsibility to the society, unshakable faith and moral intelligence.

I do my soul-work as a regular self-talk!

5. Universal Level –Commitment to self-refinement, highly correlated self-development in all you radiate what you emanate1the level, unification with the Universal Informational

You Radiate What You Emanate!

15. Conduct a Self-Restriction War - Less is More!

Naturally, self- monitoring requires a lot of will-power, self-discipline, self-control, and the ability to deny yourself the excessiveness of any sort: harmful foods, drinks, extra clothes, different odds and ends, overspending.

Change happens in a spiral upward way - two twists up and one twist back.

Sometimes, two twists back happen to block the advancement. So, you need to **mentally condition yourself with self-inductions** for consistency and success, and go through the process of constant self-monitoring with a sane head.

Eat less, talk less, fight less, and spend less!

Conduct a self-restriction war - Less is More!

Educated self-help or true **Physical Intelligence** *(Part Two, Ch. 1)* is extremely important for your health when your mind, will-power and spirit, not the doctors, are involved.

"God cures and the doctor sends the bill." (Mark Twain)

Keep intellectualizing and magnetizing your inner core - your values, culture, heart. **The cyclone derives its power from the center – your heart!** Science proves that heart is the center of the Electro-Magnetic Field in the body.

Heart is the center of your own Solar System!

Drunvalo Melchizedek, an amazingly magnifying sage of our time and a true mine of incredible information, calls it *Merkabah*, or " *The Flower of Life* "- the magnetic circle , based on sacred geometry and emanating beauty, harmony, and love that we absorb , once we make this knowledge and its restructuring effect on us our life philosophy.

Don't practice emotional starving; practice loving!

Finally, be unique, free-spirited, and magnetically–attractive! Belonging to any philosophical or religious dogma of any sort did not make the humanity any better or any happier, but personal richness, based on noble values, scientific knowledge, and critical thinking have inspired and uplifted people for centuries on end..

"Be doggedly tenacious on this path!" (T. D. Jakes)

Make Your Heart Smart and Your Mind Kind;
Be One of a Kind!

16. Accumulating Personal Magnetism

Your *self-monitoring* is a life time occupation that needs your aware attention, focused on being connected to the Universal Electro-Magnetic Field. Draw your inspiration from the universal energy source that is constantly changing your magnetic circuit of life with constructive energy of *personal magnetism.* Never giving up on your goal of raising your personal magnetism and self-consciousness being conscious at living.

Be a role model for yourself! Do not de-magnetize yourself!

Naturally, the stronger your personal magnetism is, the more life energy your magnetic circuit will get, and the more conscious your life will become.

"We are either conscious (aware) or unconscious (unaware)." (Z. Freud).

I like all the books by Rhonda Byrne, describing the magic of this law and the wonders of gratitude and love that remind us to *"count our blessings"* every morning and become more grateful and conscientious people. Charge your will-power with the main auto-suggestive booster every day.

I am a strong, calm, and determined owner of my firm will!

I can....! I want to....! And I will....!

Your conscious mind wouldn't let you get de-magnetized and go with the flow *of the common "Whatever" attitude,* **and y**ou will magnetize our inner energy core continuously, Thus, you will heighten your brain wave frequencies and increase your *psycho-tonic energy* that is driving us forward.

Body+ mind+ spirit + self-consciousness = the core of Personal Magnetism

Also, stay in synch with your personal *values and convictions* that constitute the core of your *personal integrity.* A very noble man and a great Russian writer, Leo Tolstoy wrote,

"It is vital not to be swayed by others' opinions, past thinking and doing. A personality - type man possesses his own firm convictions."

Every conscious, intelligent, reserved, kind, and compassionate deed demonstrates the unity of your mind and heart and charges personal magnetic field with *luminosity of your growing personality.*

Personal Magnetism is not What You Do;

It is How You Are!

17. Staying Young is a Life-Lasting Fun!

Aware attention to your body and to life, consciously monitored by the mind, uplifts its vibration, changing the frequencies of your thoughts, words, and feelings. It will change your entire physical state. and rejuvenate your body. You are literally becoming younger, more attractive, and more personable.

You are inseparable with your brain, or you are insane!

You can always inspire the mind to have a much longer, younger life and a more attractive appearance. When we think young, we become younger!

Enjoy a young person's bliss! Be a happy mister or miss!

When you think beautiful, you become more beautiful. **Coco Shanelle**, a great French couturier used to say,

"There are no women that are not beautiful; there are women who don't know that."

Obviously, we are what we think! The same applies to the age. In fact, we have three different ages:

1. Chronological age -   how old you are **according to your passport**.

2. Physiological age -   how old **you feel** you are,

3. Psychological age –   how old **you think** you are.

The most important age is *the psychological age*, or your thinking about your age. So, instill in yourself the program for a much younger age or for an eternal youth and keep shaping the mind-set below. It will help you stay as young as you want. Do it with the feelings of gratitude to your body and to God for the gift of life that you have, without regrets, blames, grudges, discontent, and thoughts about wasted life. It's by no means wasted if you are holding this book in your hands. Use the self-induction for rejuvenation: below:

I am 27 (pick the age …) and not a day more!

I am as young (healthy) as ever before!

I am dynamic, as ever; I am sluggish - never!

I was, I am, and I will be young (healthy) - forever!

Long Live the Beat of "So Be it!"

18. Self-Infusion Deletes Life Confusion!

Bettering yourself, do not forget *to compliment yourself* for every small victory over the pestilent bad habits.

Self-support is the inner gravity port!

The inspirational boosters will infuse your psychological stamina at each level and enhance your rational perception of life. Each time you do self-scanning, see whether you truly measure up to the *"The Best of Me!"* self-image. "We are all running on a trade mill that is set on the uphill mode." *(Reid Hoffman)*

"There is no flat ground, no security, and no compassion if you slip down.

Simply put, we never catch up because emotional stress has become a new reality that requires developing new tools of coping with it and not get off the chosen. track   Sometimes, stressful events come so fast one after another, that there is no time to recuperate. We become irritable, impatient, messy and irrational in our thinking. Dysfunctional thinking is the result of negative, uncontrolled emotions.

Only he who keeps his head will get ahead!

So, there should never be any moment in life without self-inducting and self-boosting. The basic self-induction that I have introduced above should always be at hand in your mind.

Soon negative images of self-imperfections will never happen, and intuition will prompt only positive steps to follow. With *positive self-hypnosis,* you will be able to center yourself in any situation in the Now.

I know who I am!

I am a strong, calm, and determined owner of my firm will.

I can…; I want to …; And I will…!

I am becoming better and better; kinder and kinder; smarter and smarter, etc. with each coming day.

Hurrah to me, Hurrah!

I am not Life-Negligent; I am Life-Intelligent!

19. Holistic Self - Scanning

Summing up Part Four of the book, mind you, please, that your *self-image* needs to be periodically scanned most objectively and holistically. The paradigm of *self-synthesis - self-analysis - self-synthesis* should be shaping *you* at every level of your personal growth. Do a quick snap shot of yourself continuously.

Original self-image - self-image in formation - holistic self-image

It is crucial in the process of self-molding to do self-assessment in five levels, as often as you can. Look at the mirror of your soul and do it.

"Self- creation is impossible without constant self-improvement!" (P. Pearsall)

Reflecting on what is bothering you *physically, emotionally, psychologically, mentally, and spiritually* is the way of your **active and constant rationalization** of everything that you think, feel, say, and do while processing it through the grid of conscience that plays the role of *self-attunement* to the Universal Intelligence and governess your self-acceptance.

I delete the mind's scum; I know who I am!

Self-scanning and self-monitoring, **conducted under the watch of your aware attention,** clear up the mind, calm down the emotions and focus you on the priorities in life. Old people often say that a person can sleep tight at night only if his conscience is clean. Here is an example of *a quick self-scanning* that you can always adjust to your needs. It goes from top to bottom.

1. Universal Connectedness - I am developing **intellectualized spirituality,** *the sense of Oneness with God, life and every living being*

2. Spiritual Maturity – *I imbue myself with faith, love, kindness compassion, care, grace, gratitude etc.* **My heart and the mind are in synch!**

3. Mental Awareness - *I am expanding my intellectualized awareness in five dimensions and ten intelligences and I am establishing an unbreakable bond between my heart and the mind, empowering my sub-conscious mind.* **I live consciously!**

4. Emotional Control – *I am working on my psychological awareness and emotional diplomacy. I am taming my language, controlling my emotions, and developing a strong positive attitude, patience, tolerance to every day occurrences.* **A smile, a posture, and a good mood are my emotional food!**

5. Physical Fitness – *I take charge of my body and my every cell in it, programming them for health, youth, and a happy outcome of any problem.* **I like myself the way I am!**

We Are All in the Court of the Almighty God!

20. Watch Your Mind's Torch!

Watch your thoughts
For they become your words!
Watch your words
For they become your actions!
Watch your actions
For they become your habits!
Watch your habits
For they become your character!
Watch your character
For it becomes your destiny!

If "Happiness is an Hour Long",
Be in a Hurry to have a Self-Reform!

21. For the Reader to Consider

The Second Stage of Spiritual Maturation and Soul Refinement

In sum, having gotten into the habit of constant *self-scanning, self-monitoring, and self-adjustment,* be sure to boost your spirit with the second accomplishment at *the meta-level (emotional)* of your personality-formation and self-creation.

Self-Monitoring is the form of Self-Taming!

Remember, all the levels are integrally connected inwardly and outwardly to help you sculpture yourself holistically.

The Route of Self-Resurrection:

Universal Connection	**Self-Salvation**	*Universal Dimension*
Spiritual Maturity	**Self-Realization**	*Spiritual Dimension*
Mental Awareness	**Self-Installation**	*Mental Dimension*
Emotional Control	**Self-Monitoring**	*Emotional Dimension*
Physical Fitness	**Self-Knowledge**	*Physical Dimension*

Keep developing your most personable qualities in their integral unity with all the levels of your holistic self-creation.

Self-Induction:

I Admit - I Am Emotionally-Fit!

End of Part Four - Emotional Dimension

Part Five

(Mezzo Level - Mental Dimension of Holistic Self-Development

Self-Installation

"Fertilize Your Mind with Thinking!"

(Albert Einstein)

"There is Only One Good - Knowledge and One Evil – Ignorance" *(Socrates)*

I am Not a Human Moth!

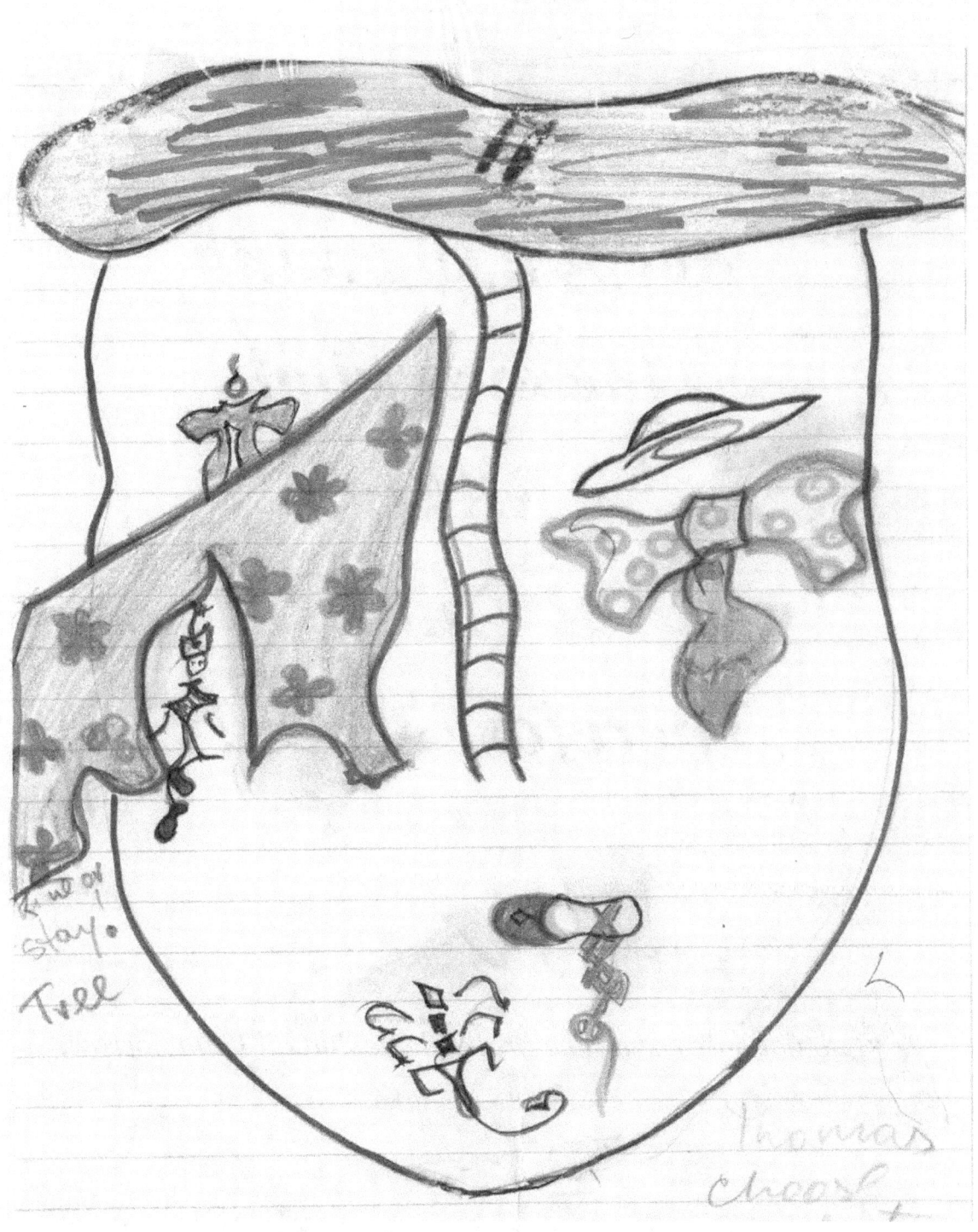

From the Birth, I Create My Own Heaven on Earth!

1. "Learning is Not Outside; It's Inside the Man."
(The Tibetan Wisdom)

Keep in the mind the ever vital RAM: "I Think, Therefore, I Am!"

Descartes)

"I do not only use all the brain I have, but all I can borrow."
(Albert Einstein)

The Art of Becoming is the Art of Mind-Monitoring!

2. The Blueprint of Intellectual Self-Growth

Self-installation is the central and the most rational part of your life, inseparable from all the rest stages of your personal growth, and it is the subject of the first book of the trilogy "Living *Intelligence or the Art of Becoming!*". No doubt, bettering yourself is impossible without ***intellectual maturity*** and trying to find your own intellectual place in the space + time bubble of life.

Not to ever fall, you need to self-install!

As a part of the Universal Intelligence, you need ***to intellectually resurrect yourself*** in the mind's spell first, and never stop doing that for the rest of your life. Getting to know the most essential information about the realities of life on the one hand, and enriching your professional intelligence, on the other, you will gain a holistic perception of life and yourself in it.

Mind is an energetic field of thought.

To self-install intellectually, you need to conquer ten basic levels of ***Living Intelligence***, presented below. *(See Introduction,1)* It is the self-development map, or the blueprint of the most essential intelligences in the same five dimensions: ***general and language intelligences*** *(physical /mini level).* ***emotional and psychological*** *(emotional / meta level)*, ***professional and financial*** *(mental / mezzo level)*, ***cultural and social*** *(spiritual / macro level)*, ***spiritual and universal intelligences*** *(universal / super level).* So, vistas of holistic intelligence are:

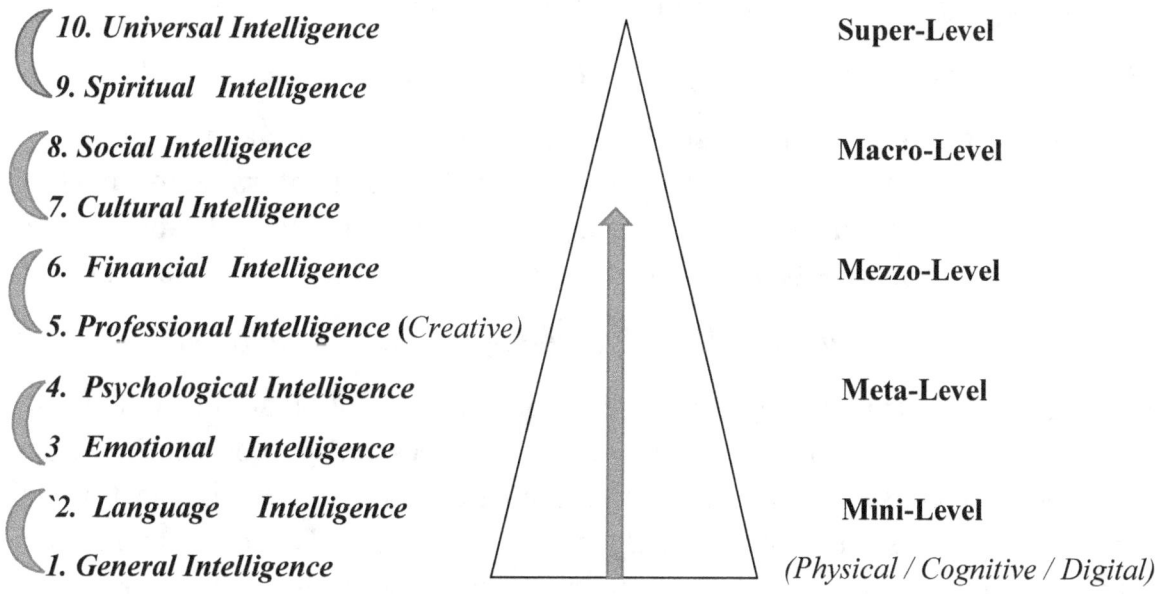

To Have a Broader Seeing,

Become a Thought-Evolved Being!

3. Holistic Intelligence and Cycles of Growth

Every level of intelligence, presented above, **has a different cognitive map,** and following it, you need to remember that the process of learning is more important than the result.

Constant intelligence re-identification is the stepping stone of self-realization!

The education that you get at school or college is great in terms of securing your future professional life. But if you become content with just this knowledge, it will very soon become **inflated intelligence**.

"Like electricity needs to be wired correctly, our souls need to be wired to the Universe by our developing intelligence." (Rev. P.S. Berg)

Living Intelligence is the education that is never complete, and it needs to be renewed with each new development in science, new reading, new reasoning, and **new life-awareness.** Ignorance, will always be a hindrance on your way, but your intelligence will delete it and dis-harm it. Be aware of the paradox of life:

The less a person knows, the more significant he deems himself to be.

So, keep learning and re-learning! Knowledge put to action is double power because action, experiment, or any idea actualization is the best test of the new information and you! Enlarge yourself with poetry, music, art, and nature. Indeed, Absolute Truth is the domain of God, and getting to know even a fraction of it is an incredible reward! According to Dr. Paul Pearsall,

"Personal productivity is not a personality trait, it's a measure of output."

The outcome of any learning must also be **connected logically** and consciously stored in the bra*in* after a thorough selection of the valid information and the deletion of the redundant one in your biological computer. Re-cycle the information that is outdated and fuse your creative skills in a non-stop fashion,

Only conscious knowledge is forming intelligence storage!

Finally, there is no true intelligence without discipline! Only disciplined, elected and structured information *(synthesis- analysis-synthesis)* constitutes true knowledge. Logical storing of the information demands conscious connecting of the past, previously sorted out knowledge with the new one. Disconnectedness of information clogs the brain pathways and generates dead knowledge and inflated intelligence. Neale Donald Walsch is more than right, saying,

"Be Conscious! Consciousness Mobilizes!"

4. You Need a Lot New Food for Thought!

Ascending the stages of *Living Intelligence*, see what intelligence you lack most and develop it in an inseparable connection with the other levels of intelligence that you have enriched your mind with.

Be more in the know of what you don't know!

The levels of intelligence are correlated **by the principle of the Russian dolls**. If one doll is missing, the inner pyramid is broken and incomplete. Even dilettante knowledge of any of the levels of intelligence, or a general idea about a certain aspect of it, builds up your holistic intelligence and expands your outlook that is crucial for your personal, **exponentially growing informational electro-magnetic field.** Your **AUTO-MEDIA** of connection with this field is charged by your constantly-renewed intelligence and the aware attention that, like the mouse on the computer, directs your mind in the right way in its search.

We get a system only where there is a structure!

The holistic paradigm of life **synthesis-analysis-synthesis** *(See Part One)* represents the intellectual process of self-installation:

Self- awareness ⟹ **self-empowerment** ⟹ **self-installation!**

Despite your best effort, you might sometimes find yourself reverting to old ways of thinking, feeling, and acting. It's a normal state of relapse that needs another **injection of will power** and **aware attention** to work through. It's also a sign from the Universal Informational Field for you to figure out what you haven't yet learned, so you could pay attention and start learning that.

Be connected to the Universal Intelligence without negligence!

Remember, the two previous stages - **self- knowledge and self- monitoring -** are the cycles of a personality growth that is impossible without a substantial intellectual fulfillment. Professional awareness, enriched intelligence, and growing self-confidence are the qualities that get solidified in you only with **expanded intelligence.** For new ideas, draw upon science, literature music, art, and nature. Albert Einstein played the violin to enhance his thought. With holistically-developed intelligence, you accumulate more and more self-worth. If any "buts" get in the way, don't hesitate to drive them off immediately with an authoritative command to the subconscious mind:

"But me no buts! Doubts destroy my guts!"

My Life Goal is to Make Myself Whole!

5. Preserve Your Mental Sanity and Individuality!

Mental sanity is our greatest asset, and preserving it is our duty. Your sanity depends on *the mental clarity and emotional equilibrium* that are based on your cerebrum that should never be unemployed! It is intelligence that installs us in life for who we are!

"Sanity is the best gift of God!" (Carl Yung)

Your subconscious mind is ruling your life, but if you focus on it your conscious mind, it makes a 360 degree turn and starts working for you, not against you. The holistic union of **body+ mind+ spirit+ sub-conscious mind+ conscious mind** *(See Introduction)* is the basis of your growing self- consciousness! So, the more you read and learn, the more constructive energy for self-installation in life you have.

"Information as a pattern of constant intelligence re-identification is the stepping stone of self-realization!" (Dr. Bruce Lipton)

The present-day turmoil of life and the ever-growing toxicity of it have increased the number of people that lose their sanity and individuality partially or completely because they are unable to follow the flood of information that sweeps them off their mental feet and pushes them on the toxic self-destruction path.

They do not re-cycle the redundant information reoccurring cycle!

It means, they do not select the information for its validity, do not strategize their lives in a better, more rationalized way, and do not reason out the lessons to learn. Therefore, they lose the ability to master e*veryday fluctuations of the positive and negative occurrences in life.* They become unable to "*reject, resist, and reform*" the chaotic and evil influences in their lives and fall victim of eventuality. Consequently, their expectations drop too low and, they settle for too little.

Chaos might suck you in, and you become its victim!

Only a person who is constantly in charge of his life behavior - his thoughts, words, feelings, actions can use negative circumstances to his advantage.

Conscious living is also healthy living!

No wonder, a psychiatrist is called a shrink in colloquial American. A good specialist shrinks your emotional and psychological display which you might be unable to control on your own. Unfortunately, a person becomes dependent on the outside help and loses his personal auto-suggestive powers.

Never Stop to Implement Your Self-Enrichment!

6. Self-Efficacy is Intelligence Based!

There is a widespread belief that individual differences in intelligence are innate and hardly modifiable. But science proves that intelligence is not fixed; it is being shaped though our lives. All it takes for a person is to become aware of his limited mental and spiritual life and have a desire to holistically expand his self-consciousness to live the life of true quality and expanded horizons of self-efficacy.

Lack of self–efficacy is the sign of self-infancy!

It's inconceivable where fundamental research and a fast-blowing technological gust might be taking us, and its horizons are so captivating that we cannot afford being depressed, indifferent, careless, ignorant, unhappy, or negligent about our self-growth.

"The secret of change is to focus all of your energy not on obtaining the old knowledge but getting the new one." (Socrates)

If you devote attention to self-improvement on a regular basis, you will give your life an impetus *physically, emotionally, mentally, spiritually, and universally.*

Intelligence is the core of self-fulfillment and self-realization.

Imagine yourself becoming empowered by a new frame of thinking that I have strategized here for you. In any situation, get the total picture of the problem, or get aware of its entirety. Next, process the problem that you need to face holistically through all the levels, selecting the level at which it should be resolved, and strategize your steps for its successful resolution. (*Synthesis-analysis-synthesis.* So, any constructive thought, idea, plan, held continuously in the subconscious mins must be brought to the conscious one and realized.

Generalize the problem + select the tactics + strategize the outcome!

It's a conscious synergetic approach that instills the mode of thinking according to which any life, business, personal relationship change has *a cyclical nature.* You are on the trade mill *of "The Best of Me!* self-image. Stay on this trade mill for the rest of your life! Only being armed with *the strategic plan of action* can you resolve any problems in life, charging your mind and your personal magnetic core with the energy of knowledge, on the one hand, and heightening *the level of self-efficacy* on the other. Self-efficacy is the key to happiness, and happiness is the key to self-efficacy. Remember the words by Socrates,

"Let him who would move the world first move himself!"

7. Being Nice is a Holistic Device!

I call this level of personality development *self-installation* because, following the beautiful words by Socrates above, you need to take full responsibility for being a personality without any reservations.

The point is, if you take care of your intellectualized spirituality, mental expansion. emotional control and physical wellness in one mindful holistic unity, the solution of any life problem will become doable. Life is based on fluctuating energy, and therefore your life vibrates between smart and stupid, good and bad, ugly and beautiful, healthy and sick, love and hatred, happiness and misery.

Life does not adjust to us, we adjust to life!

Treating life ***knowingly and respectfully***, we can consciously low down the amplitude of extreme vibrations and make them acceptable and even appreciable. We all want to be healthy, look good, be nice and sociable, recognized and loved. To look great and to be in good health, change your attitude because the mental attitude is directly related to appearance and health. Most importantly, make yourself look balanced and harmonious, not sloppy, casual, indifferent. Induct your mind with the inspirational booster: below. Balance is the Golden Section of your personality that beatifies your body, appearance and mind.

A smile, the posture, and a good mood are my emotional food!

In my life-quest, I am the best!

Have you instilled in the mind the auto-induction above? Great!

Keep being constantly self-inspiring!

Your inner climate will be reflected on your face and in every cell of your body that get stressed and become characterless, like you, letting bad vibrations and your ***poor magnetic field*** overpower them. When you are intelligent, healthy and happy, you shine. Naturally, you need to recharge your mental and emotional core, the same way as you need to charge your smart phone.

All disease is mental! Intelligence, appearance and health are related!

In line with what you have read so far, your appearance is also the indication of self-respect, or lack of any. Add the following booster to ***your emotional armory.***

Be Nice and Beautiful and beware -

There are Eyes and Ears everywhere!

8. Compliments Are Our Back-Bones!

To better yourself holistically - spiritually, mentally, emotionally, and, physically don't forget to boost your psyche and compliment yourself and others.

"I can live for two months on a good compliment." (Mark Twain)

Compliment yourself for every small accomplishment on the way of self-installation: good / better health, pleasant looks, nice words, patience and tolerance, kindness and compassion, niceness and love, demonstrated to yourself and other people. Compliments add emotional gas to our spirit's mobile and magnetize you with inspiration and self-love. Also, to envision a better scenario for your life, get rid of the phrases: *"If only…", "But I can't!" I have no time." "Whatever! "I don't care!" What do I care?* etc.

You absolutely must care for what you say and how you feel towards any situation or anyone that is on your life's path.

You are One with life and the people around you!

You're in-put into their life is reflecting who you are in the data of the Universal Informational Field that you are learning to tap with a much better quality of awareness that you have had so far. Your own informational field that is connected to the Universal one gets charged and enlightened back.

If you happen to be sick, use inspirational self-inducting to boost your immune system, delete any worries, doubts, nervousness, disbelief and fear. **Be very self-receptive and self-responsive!** Send only good information about yourself out there! Do not react to any troubles in life automatically. Structure your response according to the holistic paradigm and be sure that everything will work out.

Synthesis-analysis-synthesis!

Generalize the picture; sort out the steps to resolve the problem and strategize the positive outcome. Send the virtual message to the Universal Intelligence and start changing. The basic self-induction should always be handy in your min:

I know who I am!

I am a strong, calm, and determined owner of my firm will!

I can…! I want to… And I will…!

I am becoming better and better with each coming day!

Do Not Put a Long Face on Your Soul's Interface!

9. Moral Intelligence and Magnetism

More self-awareness is more wholeness, and therefore, **more quality of life!** An intelligent person constitutes the unity of the most important aspects of intelligence in lieu with the cosmic laws: The Law of Cause and Effect, the Law of Gravity, and the Law of Attraction, the Law of Sow and Reap. When you live in the awareness of these laws, the best human features can translate into human integrity, and you get remarkably charged in five basic dimensions of your spiritual growth., of which moral intelligence is key.

"To harvest good fruit, cultivate good thought about yourself." (*Buddha*)

Spiritual maturation	*Universal Dimension*
Morality / faith	*Spiritual Dimension*
Rationality / sex control	*Mental*
Attitude / respect	*Emotional*
Health / responsibility	*Physical*

A bad person is living under the evil effect of progressive de-magnetization and de-humanization that ruin his informational field and eventually himself.

Lack of Morality / Lack of Faith	**Super Level**
Lack of Intelligence / Ignorance	*Macro Level*
Irrationality / no sex control / Automatism	*Mezzo Level*
Negligence / Laziness / Inertia / Lying	*Meta Level*
Lack of Responsibility / poor health	*Mini Level*

To stop the downfall of a personality development is not altogether impossible, but it requires a lot of intelligence, self-monitoring and self-control. As I have indicated in Part Four, self-monitoring cultivates inner balance of morality and personal integrity. The present-day science tries to get to the bottom of *the concept of impulsivity* that breaks us in half and pushes us away from balance. To accomplish it, you must halt the unconscious, automatic way you think, balancing the life acceptance between the two extremes. In his groundbreaking book *"Robots Rebellion,"* David Icke rightfully indicates that if we go too far to the positive polarity, we lose touch with practical side of life." *Positive energy needs a negative balancer. Only balancing yourself between the two polarities of life can link you to the highest levels of consciousness."*

My Moral Make-Up is under the Thinking Cap!

10. The Path to Moral Maturity

There is no personal growth without **moral intelligence** and **moral refinement** that are inseparable with the level of a person's spiritualized intelligence and the one I keep singling out again. Moral maturation is the most challenging process because this path relates to our libido *(sexual energy)* that according to Sigmund Fraud's psychoanalytical theory is "***the driving force of all behavior,***" and it needs to be monitored by intelligence, too.

*"**Moral relativism**" (no right / wrong ethics) **is ruining our souls**."*

Moral maturation is a long process that needs to be governed from childhood. It starts with the knowledge about our procreation force and develops into an aware sense of respect for love and piety for the object of love only if it is instilled in the mind as early as possible. We cannot down-load or up-load love, we cannot delete it, block it or design it. We can only save it, and we should know how.

There is a Russian joke that a man's happiness in life depends on three types of luck: ***who to be borne by, who to be taught by, and who to marry.*** The mind and the heart in synch control the answers to the last question. Who we marry remains to be the most vital problem because the other two questions are involved with our choice of a marriage partner, on the one hand, and the chance to be either magnetized by true love and family, or become morally-demagnetized by cheating and fighting that push people off self-consciousness track.

"The further you stray from balance; the more extreme life becomes."

The right choice in marriage forms a beautiful ***habit of self-control*** that is the prerequisite for moral maturity. We must halt any images of immorality and fear of sin that harm our souls on the path of self-bettering. It's paramount to will an image of a positive moral outcome in any tempting situation with the ***stabilizing self-inductions of self-worth***.

I know who I am!

Mind you, men and women start cheating when they get tired of changing each other. Don't do that! Perfect yourself, and you will get perfection back! Neither of us is perfect, but it's very important to realize our deficiencies and correct our personal defects consciously and at the right time, not post factum. Just Sunday visits to the church will not work. Many people piously lit the candles in the church but blow off their inner light or the light of their loved ones outside the church. So, be sure to back yourself up with:

I'm Becoming Wise and Morally Stabilized!

11. Enact Your Endless Kindness Stream!

Remember, your body is the temple of your soul, and your self-sculpturing is meant to refine it and raise your consciousness to a higher level of self-freedom. To be free is also the ability to live in full accord with the people around you, the loved ones being your biggest responsibility. You are molding yourself into a conscious, holistic being, the man / woman with an advanced vision of the world, able to X-ray people for their good and bad qualities. Meanwhile, you are tolerant and kind enough to help them restructure themselves, too, **with your tactful seam of consideration and kindness** that will help patch up their personality holes.

"Every burden is a blessing!"

Once you think so about your burden, whatever it might be, the feeling of discontent, lack of character, and an unrealized selfish ambition will subside. You give yourself the foundation for love and enlarge yourself spiritually.

"Excessive ambition leads to disaster" (William Shakespeare)

You will stop blaming the other for your own misgivings and, God forbid, wasted life. Your *"The Best of Me!* self-image, instilled at the forefront of your mind, will act as a detonator. You just need to command to yourself, '*Halt*!" It will do the miracle that only self-awareness and self-respect can do. In dire situation, always remind yourself:

I know who I am!

I am a strong, calm, and determined owner of my firm will.

I can deal with…; I want to deal with…; and I will deal with…!

I am becoming *better and better, kinder and kinder….,* *with each coming day!*

Unfortunately, unpleasant situation of misunderstanding with people happen with reoccurrence because according to Albert Einstein,

"Bad habits have a good tendency.: either you kill them, or they kill you!"

Amazingly, your handling yourself thanks to auto-suggesting will immediately harmonize your inner and outer space, and help you demonstrate **Emotional and Language Diplomacy** that a real gentleman / a lady will display in any situation. *You are free to be the best / worst you could be!*

If you Want to Spiritually Reboot, be in a Hurry to Do Something Good!

12. Connect the Heart and the Mind!

I hope I have made it clear that your handling yourself *at this mental level of Self-Installation* needs to be totally conscious and mentally processed. Any trait of character that relates to your uncontrolled emotions needs to be rationalized and uploaded to your biological computer willfully. Observe your emotional intelligence without negligence! Keep inducting yourself continuously with:

Make the heart smart and the mind kind; be One of a kind!

Evolution is running over the endless barriers of obstacles, and your hurdles are quite naturally there on your personal path. The necessity to hear, feel, and understand the other in the infinite World Wide Web, or *the attitude of acceptance* of yourself and others is becoming more and more pronounced. Also, fill your heart with gratitude for what you have become, connecting your heart and the mind in *one unbreakable bond of a very noble spirit!*

There are so many inconsiderate people in our offices, among the policemen, educators, doctors, lawyers etc. To be politically correct is a required policy, and the fear to lose the job for not following it is quite natural. But we are humans and have unpredictable circumstances that require unpredictable, but considerate and compassionate responses of understanding and soul-connection. Mind you, please, when you yell at someone in an outrage of anger and discontent, you are not just let your emotional steam out, *you spit into your own soul!* Internalize the felling of disgust your soul feels and say" *Halt!* to yourself in time.

We need, indeed, the mind and heart unity to be rebuilt!

The *We-Concept* (*See Part One*) that we are developing alongside the individual identity, instills in the brain the feeling of our *mutual responsibility* for life in ourselves and others. Try to be more considerate and responsive to the people's concerns and requests, disregarding the red tape demands and acting beyond the rules when *your heart and mind in synch give you a wink.* We need to restore our mind-to-mind and heart-to heart communication, the absence of which makes us impersonal and indifferent.

The real heaven in mass is truly inside us!

"If the happiness of life is just an hour long", be in a hurry to make your heart understandingly- responsive and strong! In other words, personal and spiritual self-installation never ends! It is a life-long commitment that needs a lot of rationalization of life, self-monitoring, and self-management.

I Bring in the Sun with Me; I Walk Out with it in Thee!

13. A Meditator is the Brain Sculptor!

The auto-suggestive *self-hypnosis* that I keep reminding you of by presenting the concluding inductive boosters on every page, changes any unfavorable situation in your life. I suggest using the *Auto-Suggestive meditation* as your inspirational self-training, and I want to remind you again that it is your body's best helping hand, and any inspirational booster in this book can be the basis for such meditation. Focusing on your inner climate at the right moment, you will be raising the frequency vibrations of your entire energy field, and ***you will* flood the body with higher consciousness** every moment of your meditative self-talk. Suggestive meditation is the best way to heighten our self-consciousness.

Scientists suggest we talk to our organs and the cells, focusing our thinking on this or that organ of the body and imagining it getting warmer or cooler at will. It is called *"untactile massage."* This kind of mental massaging of any troublesome organ in your body with the power of your thoughts is very effective, and it always eases the pain in that organ, if any. You can always accompany this message with the self-inductive work:

***I can** be healthy. **I want** to be healthy! And **I** will be healthy!*

Relax completely and smile wide, enjoying the fact that you are alive. You're getting in touch with your body and overseeing your cells - your body's population - the people that you govern, ***using your biological computer - the brain.*** The auto-suggestive power of your brain is always at hand. Just upload any up-lifting booster to change your mind-set from negative to the positive

It takes only a stroke to change a minus into a plus!

Neuroscience proves now that meditation can deeply transform the adult brain through the process, called ***neuro-plasticity.*** It is the ability of the brain to adapt to our physical, mental, and emotional states and delegate different functions of the brain to its other parts, if need be". *(Michael Merzenich)* Dr. Merzenich proves that the brain is amazingly responsive to our emotional states, too.

Make brain geology work for Your Joy-ology!

I invite you to master a very simple suggestive meditation, presented in the next chapter. It will always help you put yourself together and appreciate the present moment in any situation that might get you out of balance. A person who is self-inducting is always ***responsive to the body's sensations*** and can succumb to the mind, dictating him to feel stronger, more confident, and self-inspired.

"We develop Only when We Train!" *(Aristotle)*

14. Have a Meditative Fest; Be the Best!

Below, I will walk you through such meditation. Because meditation involves consistent self-focus and the ability to zero in on your own mental state, it will also **enhance your will-power** considerably as any conscious action does.

*1. Lie flat on the back on the floor. Close your eyes and start running your **aware attention** through your body, from head to toe, to see if there is any blockage in it Breathe in deeply, inwardly saying the word" **Calm**" when breathing in, and "**down**" when breathing out. Do it consciously and very lovingly to yourself three times.*

Auto-suggestion: **Calm down, calm down, and calm down.**

*2. Next, breathe in through **the soul of your left foot**, channeling the air / energy stream along the left part of the body by its main meridian, connecting your left foot to the top of your head, right to the spot where the **crown chakra** is.*

*3. **Make a short pause at the top of the head** with your aware attention on the crown chakra and breathe out through **the soul of your right foot**, channeling the air / energy stream by the meridian on the left side of your body, visualizing it in any way that works for you (a line, a wire, a nerve etc.) After you have practiced such breathing a couple of times, you will literally feel a slight breeze at the feet when you breathe out. It's phenomenal what the mind can do! Do the same, starting to **breathe in through the right foot and breathing out through the left one.** Note it, please; you need to do the suggestive meditation in synch with your breathing Breathe in, saying inwardly the basis induction in a very **systematizing fashion.**:*

I am a strong, calm, and determined owner of my free will,

I can *be healthy, nice, polite, loving…*

I want *to be healthy,*

And I will be *healthy.*

Hold the breath for a few seconds. Start slowly breathing out, saying inwardly,

"I am becoming healthier and healthier / better and better/ stronger and stronger, etc. with each coming day!"

*5. **Repeat the auto–induction of your need three times**. You might want to do the same, breathing trough the toes of your feet, starting with the left one. Also, you may induct any mind set in this fashion. There are many of the inspirational mind-sets, written in the first-person singular for this purpose in the book at the bottom of almost every page. Finish the meditation with the self- induction below.*

Life is Tough, but I am Tougher!

15. Be Self-Re-Assessing, Not Soul-Recessing!

Concluding the Self- Installation part of the book, don't forget to synthesize your auto-suggestive work *holistically, in ten intelligences*, inducting yourself most self-lovingly at each level with what you need most at that moment from bottom to top and from top to bottom. This is the stage of the final synthesis of your self-growth at the full self-Installation level. Again, follow the *synthesis-analysis-synthesis* paradigm. Visualize the pyramid of the *Vista of Intelligence* *(See Ch. 1)* and keep it at the forefront of your mind. Monitor your breathing while doing the inductions. Below, there is an example how to do it.

I can…; (Breathe in) ***I want to…;*** *(Pause) … and* ***I will…!*** *(Breathe out)*

1. *Physical Level - I can be* healthy, radiant, happy, and content! *(I want to…, and I will …!)*
2. *Language Level – I can control* my tongue! *(I want to… and I will …!)*
3. *Emotional Level - I can be* emotionally-diplomatic, disciplined, and balanced. *(I want to… and I will …!)*
4. *Psychological Level - I can be* self-confident, unbeatable, and self-reliant. *(I want to… and I will …!)*
5. *Professional Level – I can be* professional, knowledgeable, creative, and very successful. *(I want to…, and I will …!)*
6. *Financial Level –I can be* financially-intelligent, money-disciplined, and monetary-secure. *(I want to…and I will …!)*
7. *Cultural Level - I can be* considerate, respectful, and culturally-mindful *(I want to…, and I will …!)*
8. *Social Level – I can be* sociable, friendly, and very cooperative. *(I want to…, and I will …!)*
9. *Spiritual Level – I can be* faithful, loving, kind, and giving. *(I want to…, and I will…!)*
10. *Universal Level – I can be* a real luminary, spiritually-connected, life-aware, and soul-shiny! *(I want to…, and I will …!)*

Finish your soul-infusion with the mind-set of your provisions for the future.

If my soul seeds consciously sprout;

I won't have to repeat myself a year in and a year out!

Self-Induction:

I Authenticate My Unique Self-Rate!

16. I Live Consciously!

There is only one outcome
For everyone under the Sun,
If you want to be above the ground,
Keep yourself happy and sound!

Defy the gravity of your age
With a firm and graceful rage
And accept your life in its entire mass.
For it, too, shall pass!

I Am an Active captain of My Life!
I Am Alive!

17. For the Reader to Consider

The Third Stage of Spiritual Maturation and Soul Refinement

In sum, ***having installed a much higher level of intelligence in the brain and substantially enriched your general outlook***, boost your spirit with the third accomplishment ***at the mezzo-level*** *(mental)* of your personality-formation and self-creation.

Fill up your Self-Installation quest with zest!

Remember, all the levels are integrally connected inwardly and outwardly to help you sculpture yourself holistically.

The Route of Self-Resurrection:

Universal Connection	**Self-Salvation**	*Universal Dimension*
Spiritual Maturity	**Self-Realization**	*Spiritual Dimension*
Mental Awareness	**Self-Installation**	*Mental Dimension*
Emotional Control	**Self-Monitoring**	*Emotional Dimension*
Physical Fitness	**Self-Knowledge**	*Physical Dimension*

Keep developing your most personable qualities in their integral unity with all the levels of your holistic self-creation.

Self-Induction:

I Admit - I Am Mentally-Fit!

End of Part Five - Mental Dimension

Part Six

<u>(Macro Level – Spiritual Dimension of Holistic Self-Development</u>

Self-Realization

"Every one of us has a talent for self-promotion – the energizing spark that lies within our soul." (Edgar Cayce)

Auto-Induction:

I'm a Universal Cell; I Keep Surpassing Myself!

Long Live the Belief in Yourself Without If!

To Be Physically, Emotionally, and Spiritually Alive, Raise the Spiritual Quality of Your Life!

Give Yourself a Chance to Happen!

Be the Self-Boss!

Perform Your Mission on the Planet Earth!

1. "My Life is My Mission!" *(Gandhi)*

"I Want to Desperately Live
To Internalize
What Can Be Seen
To Celebrate the Unforeseen,
To Humanize the Irreversible,
And to do the Impossible!"

(Alexander Block in my translation)

Auto-Induction:

I Want to Be and to Become!

2. Self-Realization without Frustration!

The Holistic Methodology of self-realization** th*at I am presenting to you in this book is the main concept of it because the whole book is ***the Know-how of self-realization. I am trying to put the ***form and the content*** of the book in synch as a concise and simple illustration of its ideas, following the holistic paradigm of synthesis-analysis -synthesis in every chapter. I love the rule of life.

Practice what you preach!

I am calling on you to follow this rule, too in ***your self-sculpturing*** that culminates at the level of self-realization and indicates the result of your actualization in life. Continue proving to yourself and the world,

In my life quest, I am the best!

Every person on Earth comes to life with a unique set of gifts that he / she needs to realize. Unfortunately, very many young people choose the career that is just in demand employment-wise. Thus, they betray their calling and must go through life without true self-realization, substituting their innermost goal with the expectations to get a job that will enable them to provide better for themselves.

I have come from the socialist system that, even though had its many limits, provided free and extremely knowledge-systematized education. Regrettably, it's not as good as it had been now, but the people that had immigrated from the former Soviet Union have in their intellectual store the engraved imprints of the great ***holistic education*** that makes it possible for many minds, mine included, to get successfully self-realized in the unusually competitive capitalist world.

Being holistically educated means ***having a general outlook, not just a very deep, but selectively-limited professional foundation.*** It's wonderful to have such professional insightfulness, but we also need to embrace the knowledge of the world's philosophy, literature, art, music, cultures, and religious differences as obligatory subjects, not selective ones.

Holistic education should translate into much more generalized, scientifically-insightful, and logically-built knowledge of mathematics, physics, chemistry, biology, etc. Such educational outlook may be comprised of dilettante knowledge, acquired even by self-education effort, but ***this effort needs to be inspired, motivated, and backed up.***

To Be Interesting, Get Interested!

3. Develop the Whole Brain!

I absolutely agree with Reid Hoffman who most rightfully suggests *"developing more transferable skills," the* skills and experiences of high option value -- writing skills, speaking mastery, general management experience, technical and computer skills, and international experience.

Self-realization is becoming more and more hard to obtain also because the present-day market demands *"the autonomy of thinking,"* that cannot be obtained without much more expanded horizon of knowledge that makes it possible to reach out for new opportunities, new risk-taking, and a new, holistic self-image, to begin with.

A holistically developing person has both brains - the left and the right hemisphere working in synch.

The spark of ingenuity, or an aha moment is the result of both brains creative work. We are not talking here about the difference between left -brained and right -brained people. They are well known. Creative intelligence that is also called inspiration is generated by *the whole brain* of a self-realizing person. The left and the right hemispheres of the brain work in unison, and our evolutionary development is channeling us in this direction. The people of the future, or *"the Star People."* (John Baines) are going to be whole-brained people.

When the whole brain is working, we develop **PSYCHIC SYNERGY** to better adapt to life that is not just logical but is also emotional, psychological, and social.

That's why inspired people are unbeatable and unstoppable!

To illustrate, the American Ingenuity award was given to **Leon Musk**, an amazing innovator who is rocking the world now with his innovations and most sparkling intelligence because he is amazingly holistic in his business expansion and ultimate goals' exceptionality.

"When I am concentrating on something, I tune everything else out. I am curious about anything." (Leon Musk)

The holistically creative mind gets people out of the loop of the *"immediate gratification"* of their wants and needs. They do not demagnetize themselves with material needs only, they are flying in their minds, inspiring themselves with their victories and failures that they take naturally as the fluctuations of life.

Marvel at the Grander of all and Self-Install!

4. Defy the Gravity of the Common Thought!

Accomplished people are *self-realized at every step* of their always very hard-paced and extremely challenging life on the path of the completion of their mission on Earth. They can rightfully be called "*Star People*" already because they illuminate our lives with their minds and hearts being in synch, and they manage to make our life on earth much more meaningful and synergistic. Quoting Arthur Clarke,

"The only way to discover the limits of the possible is to go beyond them into the Impossible!"

New Age thinkers speak about the necessity to develop a one-pointed mind and mindfulness that presuppose the synchronic work of both hemispheres of the brain. But to accomplish this harmonized state of the mind, you need *to discipline it and strategize it*. I have introduced above the holistic paradigm of life that I try to follow in the conceptual structure of this book, too.

Synthesis-analysis -synthesis

The world has a hierarchic structure, and it is ruled by the Universal Laws that work in synch and inseparable unity. *A man's soul is a part of the Universal Soul* as its minute cell, and the goal of each soul is, therefore, to obtain the perfection of the universal soul to be fully attuned to it. We mess up our bodies and overload our minds with redundant information, that infests our biological computers with viruses of stereotyped thinking, and lack of any drive to change the software that needs to work in one direction- synthesis -analysis-synthesis!

Generalizing + selecting / organizing + strategizing!

Clogging of our biological computers, in turn, is generating the inner havoc, emotional disbalance, and social discords. *Your goal is to protect and clean your biological computer* of the viruses of automatic thinking, laziness, lust, indifference. It is a life-long commitment that needs to be executed by an individual person working on self-salvation in life at the physical, emotional mental, and spiritual levels from bottom up and from top to bottom.

This ability *to take care of the brain's hygiene* is developed by the right brain because it is the center of idea formation, creativity, emotionality, musical giftedness and intuition. The right brain processes information holistically and momentarily, and it builds up spacious, colorful holographic images in your mind that help you become more confident, creative, and professionally exceptional

Put the Strain on Your Brain!

5. Sacred Territory of the Right Hemisphere

To self-realize on the business track of a new exponentially developing economy of global socialization of ideas is *to be religiously–committed to the methodology of the holistic self-development and its systemic paradigm*. *(Part One, Ch. 7)* Disciplined mind, a great professional awareness, and emotional diplomacy will be ruling the world of digital expansion.

So, before taking any action, *envision the scenario* of your going for it first, *select the steps* that you need to take and *instill the vision* of its successful outcome. in the mind.

In Part One , Ch 7, I am writing about the exceptional holistic qualities of Steve Jobs who was totally self-realized in life. On top of his innate holistic self-organization, *he had a real gift for team -building,* delegating the assignments to those people who had selected thoroughly and who had the same qualities of holistic vision of the idea.

Consequently, he could create *the We-Concept of* the team and instill the successful image of the outcome of the team's work in every working mind of the team. The We-concept of his team and the people's holistic work, inspired and structured by a great leadership, resulted *in the kaleidoscope of products* of the creative minds, that had employed the whole brain intelligence.

The outcome is not what you do, it's how you are!

Your creative right brain in synch with the left hemisphere will help you do it, and your intuition will fill you up with the assuredness that *the output* of your programming will be great because *the input was conscious, well selected, logically–structured and holistically strategized.*

Seek and You will find if you do not betray your heart and the mind!

Thus, you will sow your way out of any professional, or personal trouble and become the master of your destiny both personally and professionally. You will be strategizing your life better, and loving will become the second nature with you. Since love, as I have indicated above, has the neurological basis, it's mind-controlled and very inspirational. Love unifies the mind and the heart and builds up *the mental-emotional grid* for a person's inner gravity, personal magnetism, and full self-realization.

In Self-Realizing, follow the Route of

Generalizing – Analyzing – Strategizing!

6. Creative Foundation of Self-Formation!

Those of us who are insensitive, who are very emotional, and who can only talk about the necessity of self-realization are never creative. Such people do not realize that beneath the thinking process lies *the real source of creativity* which is the desire for insatiable self-expression that is Universal Intelligence-channeled.

There is no full self-realization without a creative self-expression if life.

Emotion is the bridge between conscious and unconscious minds, and inspiration to create something springs from the unity of both. Creativity is the combination of *the physical form* and *spiritual content* of the product of creation, and if both are in synch the product of creation will find its way. In the process of creation, the conscious mind is acting as the form and the sub-conscious mind, is providing the content for a goal-seeking person.

A personable man is constantly focused on the product of his creation.

That is why the power of creativity needs to be directed *willfully and holistically* at every level of intelligence-development and character-formation of a person who is dead-set on bringing his idea to life. His creative mind constantly needs new food for thought, and any new piece of information may spark *the Eureka moment.*

"I know that I know-nothing, the rest don't know even that." (Socrates)

Redundant information disturbs the mind of such people. That is why creative people are always *very vulnerable and too sensitive.* They are consciously conscious of any hostile attitude to the product of their creation.

The untrained intellect has no power over a genius mind!

Next, anyone can enhance his creative thinking by expanding the knowledge base, learning new skills, or by talking to someone outside his immediate professional network. We harness our creative potential through expanding our general outlook and a spontaneous thought that acts as a creative boost.

In sum, constantly enriched professional intelligence generates creative intelligence that develops a person's mind more than any other intelligence because it is uplifting the mind to *the Living Intelligence* level*)* that integrates all the levels of intelligence and expands a person's personal horizon holistically, charging his / her *personal magnetism* beyond words.

To Be Professionally on the Go; Stay in the Creative Flow!

7. The Holistic Culture of Ingenuity

The will to create is encoded in our DNA! Creativity is a burning sensation to let the world know about your idea and find the way to present it to the world. It's the main asset of any very good specialist with true professional intelligence and a creative mind. *Creative Intelligence* that had initially brought us to life is the unity of the rational and emotional minds. The divine spark of creativity is in everyone who realizes the need to think and feel proactively and goes beyond the limits of the possible. The air is full of ideas for the thinking mind!

RATIO + EMOTIO = PASSION OF CREATIVITY

"Creativity is ingenuity in action" (*Scientific American Mind, July 2014*). For 25 years that I have been in this country, I keep marveling at the American creativity and ingenuity. I love this country of doers and creators, of advanced minds, and intellectual and spiritual gurus. A deep well of brain potential resides within us all, but only those that keep developing their creative intelligence *"find the best way to tap into the inner savant."* (*Scientific American", August 2014*).

When we perceive something, the first thing we are aware of is sensation. Creative sensation is a very altruistic urge to better the world by contributing one's personal bit to it. Creative skills, explored by scientists, unveiled artistic capabilities of the right brain hemisphere. In 2008, a cognitive psychologist *John Koumiss* and his colleagues found that the brain activity of people who used i*ntuitive insights* differed significantly from those who preferred the analysis or used the left brain's capabilities. This study, along with Carson's reports from highly creative individuals, suggest that *"we can prompt the brain to create,"* employing both hemispheres in a holistic unity to produce the impossible.

"You should first wander the world with an open mind!"

Curiosity and imagination develop our creative right brains. The right hemisphere of the brain is responsible for our ability *to generalize, to select, and to infer,* following the holistic paradigm **SYNTHESIS-ANALYSIS-SYNTHESIS**. These three basic skills develop the right part of the brain with the help of visualization, listening to classical music, beautifying our speech, enriching the vision of beauty and harmony around us, and *synergizing* our lives and the lives of the people that we come in touch with. Indeed, every country of the world contributes for the general evolution of the humanity, producing new amazing testimonies of human creativity. As Albert Einstein put it,

For knowledge to be useful, it must be Creatively Applied.

8. Financial Awareness

The form and the content of the world economy are changing exponentially, and our *financial awareness* transforms with it, too. ***Professional, creative, and financial intelligences*** are the domains of a personality growth on the path of obtaining personal freedom, propelling the ability to self-realize in life.

The best of me is financially free!

Financial Intelligence is an integral part of s personal growth and self-actualization. In the Introduction, I am talking about the change in the paradigm of self-realization, accentuating ***being over having***.

However, money is the tool that a self-developing person needs ***to operate consciously*** because lack of financial independence hinders the process of self-creation financially that should not be blind or patterned by other business endeavors. In other words, ***money needs brains!***

To climb up the financial hills, develop your money-management skills.

Financial skills is what you need to obtain as early as possible, too. All the most realized people started with developing their *financial awareness* very early on, building themselves and their businesses from scratch thanks to financial intelligence and risk -taking that always go hand in hand. Researchers have found that there is a gene, linked to credit cards debts. Emmanuel De Nave writes,

"A particular gene affects our financial behaviors"

Here we go again. As Dr. Lipton claims, *(See Rationale, Ch. 7))* genes do not rule the brain, cells do.so, we need to teach our cell financial intelligence. Presumably, you have already mastered your general, language, emotional, and psychological arrays of knowledge, ascending your awareness in ***the mini-meta, mezzo, macro, and super levels.*** Financial skills need to be developed exponentially in these five levels, too. your holistic thinking is supposed to build the stairway fro your business and money policy.

Knowledge is power, knowledge put to action is double power!

I have already presented my philosophical assessment of Steve Job's phenomenal success *(Part One, Ch. 7),* based on ***the unanimity of the form and concept*** of his creative genius and his following the universal paradigm of holistic thinking.

Synthesis-analysis-synthesis.

I this level of your intellectual and spiritual evolution, you need ***to live by the professional code*** that every one of us needs to work out for themselves in accordance with the calling of his heart that is the center of the personal information field. As a matter of fact, ***strength is not muscles, it's a strong heart,*** charged by the goal of self-realization professionally, financially and personally because both professional and financial intelligences are the ***unity of knowledge and skills*** that each mind develops on his / her own.

Manage the money knowingly, too, to become a financial guru!

In sum, professional intelligence is a life-long commitment, the same as self-development. Recognition should be given again to the book *"The Start-up of You"* by Reid Hoffman and Ben Concha because they view the present-day professional development in a very actionable way.

"To adjust to the needs of a fast-developing market,
you need to invest into yourself."

Professional intelligence is not a stagnant phenomenon because it requires a lot of professional awareness that is the present-day platform of business communication.

Intelligent, creative, and personable workers that demonstrate professional and financial awareness in business and communicate with business associates on the basis of **aware attention** + **mind-to mind** + **heart-to-heart basis** are guaranteed to be overly successful.

Don't Be Money-Negligent; Be Money-Intelligent!

Self-Induction:

My Professional Vigor is at a Trigger!

9. Don't Let the Negative Stuff Occupy Your Mind's Gulf!

(An Inspirational Booster)

Don't let the negative stuff
Suck you into the evil gulf

Of disbalance, depression,
Fear, anger, or any obsession

That take minutes and hours
Days, months, and years- sprouts

Off your life's calendar biz
With its obtrusive trapeze

Together with money being wastefully spilt,
It adds the volume of self-guilt!

So, to be better life-standing
Get also rid of indecision and misunderstanding!

Your Life Equation lies in the Spiritual Invasion!

10. Be Self-Monitored, Not Society-Programmed!

The mind of a thinker always opens the door into the Universal Intelligence and works in tight cooperation with it, becoming *Living Intelligence in action.* Living intelligence is very personable and integrated too. It requires non-stop designing and re-designing of Self!

It means you are shaping yourself into a leader!

The problem is, people are either unable or unwilling to make hard decisions and to bring about real changes that provide a vision and the strategy for their implementation. *Our managerial culture lacks professional intelligence.*

It turns out we have a lot of managers everywhere, but very few real leaders that not only decide smarter and hit more lucrative targets, but change the framework of business, science, and life overall. Senior management often cultivates the culture of fear when people are afraid to express their thoughts which could have changed the texture of any enterprise

Being aware of such situation, you should always feel free to demonstrate your *professional competence* and *financial awareness,* expressing yourself freely, without red-tape restrictive obstructions. Choosing not to speak up or do anything in the face of obvious impossibilities fades your talents and deletes the possibilities. Turn on your mind's uniqueness and enthuse yourself with confidence. Someone said,

"When I am right, nobody remembers, when I am wrong, nobody forgets."

That so true! Your new ideas may seem bold and unrealistic, **but you know better.** You are the one who is on permanent communication with **the Universal Intelligence**, and the one who can infiltrate the environment with his creative his thinking and give the world the best he has. It is guarding you in the implementation of your "crazy" ideas and makes you **defy the gravity of a common thought**. Suddenly, the idea starts shaping you!

"For an idea that does not at first seem insane, there is no hope.' (Einstein)

Most importantly, don't knock yourself out trying to compete with others. Build yourself up competing only with yourself and developing yourself into a fully-grown, *mature individual* with his own mind and scale of values, and, most importantly, *a high level of consciousness* that is always based on personable qualities of exceptionality. I love these words by Steve Jobs very much:

"Try? There is No Try, only Do, or Not Do!"

11. Inertia of Thinking, Speaking, and Acting

We live in a technologically sophisticated universe, and your total realization in life is possible if you learn to constantly *re-engineer your thinking,* making it go in the flow with the latest advancements in science and technology, turning it into *pro-active thinking,* not reactive thinking.

Inertia of thinking, speaking and acting pushes you into the trap of reacting.

Proactive thinking is conscious, responsive. and purposeful. On the path of full self-realization and self-salvation., you are learning to channel your thinking holistically, in full accord with the cosmic law of "The *Cause and Effect."* that is governing the thinking and actions of self-conscious and advanced minds.

Be wise, let the cosmic laws give you advice!

Tune yourself up to the Universal Intelligence as often as you can to listen to the inner voice of your professional and personal intuition. Purposeful thinking, speaking and acting are the signs of developed self-consciousness, the one that is in accordance with the cosmic *Law of Sow and Reap* that people disregard very often, being on the automatic drive in life.

"The one guiding his mind protects his life." (Proverb 13,3)

You should not overlook the Cosmic Laws in any situation. Learn to deal with any problem with *full awareness* of the reasons that have generated any problem. Reasonable, connected thinking is formed as the result of *conscious thinking.*

Think consciously, work consciously, self-realize consciously!

To get to a new dimension of spiritualized consciousness, we also need to operate with the problems in the most conscious way because *the professional world is also being screwed up by automatic, thoughtless job functioning*. Brain-wracking is an exercise for purposeful thinking in the search of the solution of any problem, with full commitment and an activated self-efficiency.

"Put your mind on fire: be proactive!" ("The Start-up of You")

The obtained academic degrees and tenues are often in the way of a person's further professional and scientific growth. It happens because we generate certain *stereotyped mental habits* that condition our thinking and make the mind inflated with worked-out patterns. Not to fall into the trap pf patterned thinking, Reid Hoffman suggests,

"Never Leave a Start-Up's Mind Position!"

12. What's Yours is Limitless!

There is nothing compared to the feeling of a single accomplishment on the path of self-evolution. You attain the super power over yourself which is the greatest accomplishment of all. People start gravitating to you in hope to gain some inner strength that you emanate because true personality development goes beyond one's professional credentials.

It's your personal, unique know-how!

Over the years, every true professional accumulates unique knowledge, sorts out the information in his /her mind storage and develops *exceptional skills* that no one can take from him / her because the complete framework of the thought-process of its owner is beyond anyone's reach. Therefore, the banal statement," ***Everyone is replaceable!*** " is evil in its core because exceptionally talented, giving and personable people cannot be replaced! They are innately unique!

"A genius is a man who realized his mission in life." (Goethe)

That is why, even in the cases of the intellectual theft, the intellectual property cannot become totally plagiarized. Any idea that you might have voiced out, or even published, cannot be taken completely by someone ready to pick up somebody's mind. You can be robbed of it partially, but it will never be realized in the way you see it yourself, in its unique totality, or holistically.

So, do not limit yourself with the fear of plagiarism.

Your professional mind is an endless source of ideas when it keeps operating with confidence in its uniqueness. It penetrates the essence of other disciplines and gets to the hidden causes of all that is manifested as an effect in your own area of expertise that remains to be unique. Such situation proves Norbert Winner's brilliant observation about today's professional world when we need to send a person that is seeking the solution of a small professional problem" ***to the next door down the corridor,***" instead of dealing with it then and there.

As a matter of fact, all you need is a holistic visualization of the problem and its immediate X-raying for the trouble-spots to be selected and removed. Strategize your actions after that and be sure that this approach presupposes the possession of ***a real, your personal know-how*** that will propel your confidence and professional success. success.:

"Don't be just the Best, Be the Only!"

(Steve Jobs)

13. Professional Consciousness

Belief in oneself, backed up by **Professional Intelligence** becomes practice. Practice becomes professional awareness. ***Professional awareness becomes professional competence.*** Professional competence becomes professional consciousness! Heightening of *professional consciousness is an on-going process* now, and it needs a flush of new, fresh **professional intelligence.**

Professional consciousness is a deep, responsible understanding of the consequences of the implementation of your idea, for the good or bad of the people, their health, education, happiness, and life. A great Russian writer and a doctor, Anton Chekov said,

"If you cannot help, don't harm!"

It is known that Albert Einstein had signed a letter, written by the Hungarian physicist Mr. Szilard, sent to the United States President Franklin D. Roosevelt in 1939, warning him that Germany might develop an atomic bomb. Later, he regretted signing that letter because it led to the use of the atomic bomb in Japan.

Professional consciousness is directly connected to professional conscience.

Unfortunately, there are numerous examples in our history, dealing with the poor professional consciousness, dimed by the money chase. However, a noble personality will pursue the goals of common good, and we should raise such people in our colleges. Such approach requires mastering of the chosen profession, based on holistic, ***constructive, and disciplined thinking*** together with ***a noble aspiration"*** to give the world the best we have."

Bold intelligence of such people, whose imagination goes beyond the accepted norms, change themselves and the world. History abounds in stories about amazing geniuses that went far beyond their educational limits, questioning the impossible and evolving the world with their incredible answers to it. The holistic route of their self-realization is, was, and will be:

Internalizing-Personalizing-Externalizing!

The giants of professional intelligence, such as Steve Jobs, Bill Gates, Alan Mask, and many technologically-advanced minds are the example of extreme brain organization, discipline, independent thinking and constructive, strategic vision, that is always on the brink of the impossible. *(See Preface, Ch. 1,2)*

I can…! I want to…! And I will…!

I Am Living Intelligence in Action!

14. Professional Self-Assessment

Professional self-reflection is the guarantee that you will never fall behind in your knowledge and skills when knowledge becomes inflated and skills get rusty. Constant work at both is the necessity because a real professional must have them in synch, especially during our digital exponentially- changing times.

Knowledge + skills = the flow of professional and personal life!

You can make your own **list of guidelines in five dimensions** that will reflect the levels of your professional growth, depending on the profession or the job that you are practicing. Quiz yourself to build more professional confidence and fortify your professionalism with awareness, sense of measure and objectivity.

A sense of measure is a great mind's treasure!

Professional wisdom means that you do not think reactively; you think pro-actively. The usual sharpness is not of value here. Insightful, slow, digestive and purposeful thinking in five dimensions is a must in such cases. So, you need to expand your thinking beyond the common smartness to the professional wisdom holistically! I have raised my son in this wisdom, and he became a world class businessman of an incredibly-successful content.

Holistic professional intelligence means effective, pro-active, not reactive thinking. The critical use of intelligence is required when our job situations demand that we generate new context, concepts, solutions of problems, and set up new objectives. Nowadays, the brain storming technique is not enough in many cases. We need the tandem of *new professional awareness + aware attention skills.* Effective thinking must be based on the *conceptual analysis of the problem on five levels,* channeled by aware attention in a holistic way, both tactically and strategically.

I call such thinking **Channeled Thinking** because it is channeled by aware attention that is actualized as the scanning tool in the solution of a problem in the five holistic dimensions. Thus, you will get better aware of the *competitive advantages"* (Reid Hoffman) and raise your unbeatable business assets. Actualizing such holistic skills, you will finally acquire the highest professional consciousness, and with it, a promotion or the desired financial reward will inevitably come. Also, compete only with yourself. Envy creates a gap within you. Don't fall into it! If such emotions hit you, drive them off auto-suggestively:

I don't fall into an envy cell; I compete only with myself!

I am a Unique Cell; I Keep on Surpassing Myself!

15. "Be the Thing in Yourself!"

I see the philosophical statement of a greatest German philosopher, Immanuel Kant in the title of this chapter as the representation of the content and form unity of any phenomenon. If you view self-formation as a life-realization goal, the inseparable unity of your **physical form and mental content,** you will become *"the thing in itself."*

"Only such oneness completes a person as a subject of the world.".

Kant calls the wholeness that builds up personal integrity **"*the thing-in-itself,*"** and such integrity makes a person self-reliant and self–sufficient. It is the prerogative of having fewer failures in life and more successes. ***Self-sufficiency*** and ***self-efficiency*** are great prerequisites for self-installation in life. Also, it's essential not to verbalize everything that comes to the mind. Let the idea ripen there first. The wisdom of by Robert Shulle is great to remember here.

Don't be simple-hearted about your success in front of people,

only in front of God!

Your inner wholeness and optimism will make your mind and psyche enthused. You will become the happiest man / woman on earth because you have a purpose in life that keeps you going on, without being hampered by anyone's judgment or skepticism. An optimist lives in a self-created bliss because his world is never stagnant. "Follow Dr. Paul Pearsall's advice,

"Feed your faith in success and doubts will starve to death!"

You should always be aware that your head creates your world! It takes time to get to know oneself better in the world of non-stop creation that abounds in failures. Failures are the short-cuts to self-awareness and self-confidence. Unfortunately, when we fail on our trial and error path, we allow others to drain us of our enthusiasm and the belief that the right decision is just around the corner.

Manage yourself to handle your ideas and people better!

Great minds teach us to clear the residual emotions and see the roots of our failures in their three-fold transformational capacities:

1. Find yourself!   *2. Motivate yourself!*   *3. Commit yourself!*

"To be a Creator in Hell,

I must Believe in God and Myself!" *(Ben –Groin)*

16. Professional Intelligence Auto-Suggestively

To finalize my schematic presentation of a very conceptually rich topic, I'd like to present a few main tips on how to help you attain more will-power in self-realization auto-suggestively. Mind you, in a psychologically-challenging situation, you need to provide *an* inner vacuum for new psycho-tropic energy – ***the main energy of the spirit.***

The greatest energy remains to be the energy of the unbreakable spirit of Thee!

1. To begin with, ***you should stop thinking of your imperfections as unchangeable***. The wisdom of real personality transformation lies in the changeability or impermanence of our misgivings. Once you come to grips with the state of your **general self-management**, the rest will become a piece of cake.

In my life quest, I am the best!

2. In a conflicting situation, relax and picture **"The Best of Me!" holistic pyramid.** *(Part Two, Ch. 9)* that, I hope, you have placed on the wall a visual reminder of your self-installation in life. Stay away from negative, critical colleagues, friends, and loves ones. They only ***drain you of the psychotropic energy*** that you need to empower yourself with auto-suggestively:

I don't want to be ever told about my imperfect personal mold!

3. Self-realization generates the feelings of contentment and kindness in us. The spiritual teachings tell us that to feel better, we should help someone. Kindness is a dose of anti-hostility, anti-depression, and anti-self-pity. display it everywhere!

Make your mind kind, and your heart smart!

4. Take care of your professional appearance and be sure to radiate light and warm up your outer space with ***a nice, synergistic personality.*** Look psychologically invulnerable and professionally confident! Induct yourself with the main inspirational booster, or any self-induction that comes to mind. Your happiness depends on yourself and your **AUTO-MEDIA** that should never fail to induct you with self-confidence and self-efficiency.

I know who I am!

I can…1 I want to…, and I will…!

I am becoming more and more impenetrable / confident / self-sufficient / self-reliable / unbeatable / unstoppable etc. now! I am great! Wow!

I Never Whine; I Shine!

17. Infuse Your Self-Realization Fuse!

(An Inspirational Booster)

Every day, when you are without any mask,
You must address yourself and ask,

"What have I done today
For my physical array?

Have I added a bit
To my emotional upbeat?

Have I enriched
My mental out-reach?

And, finally on the spiritual plane,
Have I gotten closer to God's domain?"

So, don't waste your daily zest
To just possess

Use it to infuse
Your self-realization fuse!

Your Life's Goal is the Aristocratism of the Soul!

18. Victory Over Yourself is Your Magic Spell!

When you failed to do something, the first question should be not where the mistake lies, but *why* the mistake had occurred in the first place. It is at your fingertips to regenerate the action that had failed and channel your thinking toward success in it. Such attitude speaks of the change of consciousness.

" Falling does not make you a failure but staying down does." (Napoleon Hill)

These words are exceptionally important for a person on a self-realization path. Successes are natural fluctuations of positive creative intelligence. So, you must constantly control your thinking and your belief in yourself. The degree of your success depends entirely upon your **ability to restore the inner light of self-confidence** and better the situation with your magnetic auto-suggestive in-put.

.A Smile, a posture and a good mood are my magnetic food!

With any negative action, you are putting ourselves at risk of de-magnetizing yourself. Without conscious control of what your mind is working at, you are doomed to walk all your life on the cyclical treadmill of *success –failure*. You must have personal determination to participate in the process of self-actualization and do everything required for it at any time and in any place. As a famous business philosopher Jim Rohn puts it,

"If you must be addicted to something, make it an addiction to winning!

Winston Churchill had to start from scratch four times, and each time he taught himself to take every failure with more calmness and acceptance, generating more confidence and faith in God and himself. He kept saying to himself, **"Don't be vexed, be humbled."** Doubt poisons all endeavors and generates *the immobility of thinking* that is the malady of people in trouble. Doubt is, in fact, part of life if we view life as the field of energy that is fluctuating in a negative / positive fashion, exactly as our personal lives do.

"Productivity is not a personality trait; it's a measure of your life's output!"

In sum, change the cognitive map of your self-development daily. Enrich your mental store with new knowledge tirelessly because there is no limit to knowing. The process of learning is much more important than the result because it also. pushes the possibility of the Alzheimer disease far from your life track.

A New Form and the Content of Thee is

What Everyone Should See!

In the Name of Christ,

Don't Ever Whine; Soil-Refine!

19. I Am My Own Best Friend!

(Mental Trip One)

Concluding the auto-suggestive work at the spiritual, **SELF-REALIZATION** level, it is always a good idea to summarize the work done and to assess the progress of your inner work and self-modification in the most positive way. Keep inducting strength and perseverance into your spirit:

Life is tough, but I am tougher!

There are many very persuasive auto-suggestions provided in my book on intelligence *"Living Intelligence or the Art of Becoming."* They are provided at every level of your self-programming. In this part of the book, we present five very simple mental trips *to* back up your emotional uplift that you have experienced, most surely, having read the book that far. Every one of us needs a ***mental, emotional, physical and psychological support*** - the support in self-respect and self-modification. We all get constantly criticized by our parents, the loved ones, friends, bosses, and the people who know nothing about us, but who judge us, anyway, and who give us grades for our looks, manners, speaking, working, and just being everywhere.

Beware; there are eyes and ears everywhere!

There is only one person who always supports us, backs us up in trouble, justifies us for the mistakes we make, understands us like no one else, and who feels pain when we cry and joy when we are happy. This person is **YOURSELF**! Remember, your main auto-induction is:

I am my best friend; I am my Beginning and my End!

Only I know how great I am and how very special I can be!

I do not want to be a clone of anyone;

I am quite happy with who and what I am!

If Anyone Doesn't Like Me,

It's His or Her Problem, not Mine!

20. The Ultimate Picture of Me!

(Mental Trip Two)

Since I am constantly sculpturing myself, I am proud of being Me! Here's what I am, and I can be!

*1. I'm (state your age here) **years young!***

2. I'm healthy, good-looking, and well-mannered!

3. I'm kind, nice, and positive!

4. I'm strong, courageous, and characterful!

5. I'm intelligent, rational, and broad - minded!

6. I'm independent, self-reliant, and self-sufficient!

7. I'm hard-working, competent, and efficient!

8. I'm patient, tolerant., and reliable!

9. I'm ambitious, hard-working, and very motivated!

10. I am determined, decisive, and aspiring!

11. I am loved, loving, and caring!

12. I am respected, appreciated, and rewarded!

I am aware of my ***physical, language, emotional, psychological, professional, financial, cultural, social, spiritual, and universal*** growth *(See Part One, "Vistas of Intelligence")* because:

1. My weight is normal.

2. My clothes are fitting and matching me.

3. I like the way I look.

4. My job is rewarding me.

5. My confidence is growing.

6. I depend only on myself.

7. I manage my life! I AM ALIVE!

Life is Going on, and It's Beautiful in its Every Form!

21. I Can! I Want to! And I will!

(Mental Trip Three)

To move toward a Better Me, I need more *energy* and **motion**, I need more

E-Motion!

To attain more emotional energy every time that my mood or my spirit sag for whatever reason, I immediately fill my mental-emotional tank with my *every day auto-suggestive gas:*

I am a strong, bold, calm, and determined owner of my firm will!

I can
I want to, — be *in charge* of my thoughts, words, feelings,
And I will
and actions!

I am becoming better and better at……
with each coming day!

I am in Love with Self;
I Keep Surpassing Myself!

22. I Won't Go Afore; I'll Will My Life More!
(Mental Trip Four)

I Eat, Talk, and Spend Less.
I Have a Self-Limitation War;
I Will My Life
More!

"Under Any Circumstances, Always Do Your Best,
No More and No Less!"
(Don Miguel Ruiz)

23. Self-Affirming is Character-Forming!

(Mental Trip Five)

You can never overdo the work at bettering yourself, for it's never enough! When time allows, you need ***to strategize your self-growth*** by way of systematizing the result of the work done in the Present Perfect Tense that signifies the result of the personality growth action. It's very satisfying to get an inward boost of Information selection, a desired result. It helps to attain it without fail! ***Direct the laser beam of your aware attention to your innermost self.*** Do self-affirming consciously and with self-respect and assuredness.

I know who I am!

I Can…! I want to …! And I will…!

I am a strong, calm, and determined owner of my free will!

----

1. I've transformed myself into the Whole Me! I am as good as I could ever be!

2. I am not doing things in a robot-like trance. I am governed by my aware attention dance.

3. I've managed to discipline my thoughts, words, emotions, and actions! I raise my words, not my voice!

4. I've developed a synergetic win-win mentality; I've turned hostility into humility.

5. I am not listening to people with pseudo-attention; I am in my aware dimension!

6. I hear everything that is said to me, and people hear me out, too.

7. Love is my life's mold; I've learned to love by the moral code!

8. I am happy, no matter what! Happiness is my every day job!

Finish your self-induction with the mind-set at the bottom of this page. It is good to be remembered in any emotionally-charged situation.

Self-Induction:

I Make My Heart Smart and My Mind Kind.

I'm One of a Kind!

24. In My Life Quest, I Am the Best!

Life is just a moment

Of our dissolution

In everyone and everything

As a gift of self-solution!

Self-Induction:

Long Live the Belief in Myself without If!

25. For the Reader to Consider

The Forth Stage of Spiritual Maturation and Soul Refinement

In sum, *having raised your professional intelligence, realized your creative potential, and accomplished spiritualized intelligence,* be sure to boost your spirit with the accomplishments *at the macro-level (spiritual)* of your personality-formation and self-realization.

In my thought, I report only to God!

Remember, all the levels are integrally connected inwardly and outwardly to help you sculpture yourself holistically.

.:

The Route of Self-Resurrection:

Universal Connection	**Self-Salvation**	*Universal Dimension*
Spiritual Maturity	**Self-Realization**	*Spiritual Dimension*
Mental Awareness	**Self-Installation**	*Mental Dimension*
Emotional Control	**Self-Monitoring**	*Emotional Dimension*
Physical Fitness	**Self-Knowledge**	*Physical Dimension*

Keep developing your most personable qualities in their integral unity with all the levels of your holistic self-creation.

Self-Induction:

I Admit - I Am Spiritually-Fit!

End of the Part Six - Spiritual Dimension

Part Seven

(Super Level - the Universal Dimension of Self-Development)

Self-Salvation

)

"To conquer others is to have power; to conquer yourself is to know the way." (Tara Rae)

I Propel My Awe of Thought to be Worthy of God!

The Super-Conscious Mind is what I Must Unwind!

I am developing the Super-Conscious Mind;
I am One of the Kind!

1. Change Your Life's Algorithm to Self-Enthusiasm!

If You Live in the Sun, No one will Do You Any Harm!

So, Be in Unity with Your Inner Divinity!

"The one that found himself is like the Sun!"
(A Japanese proverb)

In My Thought, I am One with God!

2. Become Spiritually Aristocratic, not Bureaucratic!

The Universal Intelligence is the top intelligence! No doubt about it. Spiritual intelligence makes us shine from inside. However, we cannot just declare that we are spiritual beings; we should earn this title with demonstrating our ***personal spiritual integrity.*** As I have stated many times so far, spiritual development is the most important stage on the way of self- salvation because the search for God is eternal and innate in all of us. The urge for unattainable perfection has been driving human beings on the way of evolution for centuries. So, the statement," ***Nobody's perfect***" is banal and meaningless because it is used just to justify the weakness of going with the flow.

Religiousness is a Choice; Spirituality is the Inner Voice!

As per science, *"the Americans are the most sinful nation on earth"*. *(Scientific American mind< 2013)* Fun and money chasing are killing the minds and souls of people and prioritizing material success and fun life. Moms tell the kids heading to school, "***Have fun!*** Later, after they come home from school, they ask them, "***Did you have fun?***" Isn't it indicative of a wrong orientation for kids who, unfortunately, seek fun afterwards everywhere, prioritizing the search for money and fun for the rest of their lives?

Being spiritually aristocratic is a new and very challenging responsibility!

Transforming yourself intellectually, you develop new thoughts, feelings, convictions, values, and aspirations. You generate new abilities to love, to forgive and to forget. You are ascending the stairs of evolution, the state at which you consciously realize that the higher the level of your self-consciousness, the more care it requires to survive in our cruel, impersonal world!

It's difficult to climb the stairs to Heaven, but very easy to slide down to hell!

To be true to what we all preach, we must acknowledge that ***it's a conscious and willful process*** that often remains just words, not actions. The point is, it is literally impossible to attain spiritual intelligence without enriching intelligence and refining the soul at all the levels holistically and exponentially.

The motivation to be spiritual grows inside the person, level by level.

In sum, spiritual intelligence is the top of personality development. With the inner current directed toward God, your life will have a renewed quality, depending on the state of your consciousness that is ascending together with your personality.

"God Helps those who Help Themselves!"

3. Spiritual Maturation is Our Self-Salvation!

We are all sharing the same Universal Consciousness, evolving our intelligence and enriching our spirituality. However, our evolving consciousness should not be just religiously mechanical, it needs to be intellectually-deep, insightful, aware, unshakable, and eternal! As Dr. Fred Bell write,

"Spiritual aristocracy begins with the individual and ends with him."

Every sacred book is unfolding the human mind **on physical, emotional, mental, and spiritual levels** that I have outlined above in terms of developing the most personable traits of character, helping you to be the best in the life's quest.

The whole field of life is glorified by our taking care of **being the best at each stage!** Our common goal is to develop **the Super-Conscious Mind** on these levels holistically. We're all guided by the values generated by God, but we live by the standards that are shaped by our intelligence and the cultural environment that frames our current values that are often self-centered, not God-centered. *As Edgar Cayce writes,*

"What you think, what you put in your mind, to work upon, to live upon, to feed upon, to live within the mind –that is what you become in God.

That is Law!"

So, when talking about **spiritual maturation,** and I do not give preference to any religion. All religions are interpretations of the eternal concept of creation - the God that is viewed by science now as **"a Universal designer".**

"Man may produce the stumbling stones; God alone-in the mind of man may make them stepping stones." (Edgar Cayce)

All sacred books contain the laws of life that are conceptually built and authentically illustrated with respect to our cultural differences, but **the core of all them is One,** and it is the main prerequisite for our future unavoidable spiritual unification. As intelligent human beings, we are supposed to process the meaning of the Universal Laws on our own because only an individual person is responsible for his / her spiritual growth, not the priest, not any spiritual authority of any rank, not even the Pope. Churches are mushrooming as businesses around the world; the congregations of religious people are growing, too, but the level of our spirituality is hardly rising. Obviously, each one of us needs to manage their own inner currents intelligently, consciously, and individually.

I Can Roam any Terrain with God in My Vein!

4. Spiritual Wellness is in Wholeness!

Self-realization is instrumental in self-salvation! Our whole life is the process and the result of both. Once you have managed to self-express the unique urge to give the world the best you have, you have installed yourself spiritually as well.

This is the most uplifting feeling of all to be completely self-installed!

I am sure you have met the self-realized people that are shining from inside with the inner light of holistic intelligence, personal integrity, professional and moral wholeness, and incredible charismatic magnetism. They have accomplished self-development in physical, emotional, mental, and spiritual levels. They have developed **high self-consciousness** and accomplished material security.

Body + Spirit+ Mind (sub-conscious +conscious minds) = *high self-consciousness!*

The super level of self-development is indeed the level of s*uper intelligence and super consciousness,* the level of the highest godliness and nobleness that a human being can accomplish during his life time. It is the level of the saints that human history has produced as the best Luminaries of the world. Like **the Golden Section** that defines perfection, but remains infinite in its unattainable completion, we need to be led by the infinite idea to become better, better, and better to come closer to the Source of all Creation – God.

On our realistic everyday life's plane, we, too, need to aspire for unattainable perfection, and therefore, a banal comment, *"No one is perfect"* is just a weak justification of a characterless person. Keep forwarding your personality creation upward against all odds. Finally,

a) you will *break free from your old habits;*

b) you'll *establish quantum communication with the Universal Mind through your* **AUTO-MEDIA;**

c) you will start *reading into the meaningful coincidences* in your life;

d) you will *develop a mind-to-mind contact with the Universal Intelligence* and establish a telepathic connection with other people on earth. *The synchronicity* of such happenings will increase because you will be in touch with the Universal Mind through your intuition and acute conscience all the time.

"The Only Way is to Go Up into God and Down into Yourself!" *(Dalai Lama)*

5. Stages of Wellness are the Stages of Wholeness!

Being **WHOLE, OR SPIRITUALLY- MATURE** also means being complete at every level of life because life is complete, whole, and inseparable. A healthy body is impossible without a healthy spirit, and a healthy spirit is residing only in a healthy body. Both are the manifestation of the level of consciousness that you achieve during self-development.

Stages of Wellness are the Stages of Wholeness:

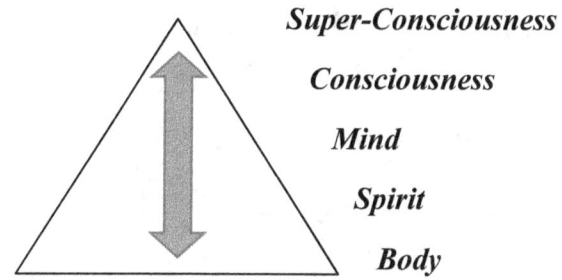

Super-Consciousness	*Universal wellness / wholeness*
Consciousness	*Spiritual wellness / wholeness*
Mind	*Mental wellness / wholeness*
Spirit	*Emotional wellness / wholeness*
Body	*Physical wellness / wholeness*

Our wellness is our wholeness, and our wholeness is our wellness!

Life is becoming more complicated and challenging, more hectic and overwhelming with each day. The present-day turmoil creates a havoc at every level of life and, naturally, we cannot fix one area without trying to deal with the others because the holistic paradigm which we need to follow now demands such integrity.

Body + spirit+ mind+ consciousness + sub-consciousness = Super-Consciousness!

To mobilize ourselves for the speed of life and to go with the flow in it, we need to bring **a tremendous organizational contribution** to this paradigm (*synthesis-analysis-synthesis*) and perform **SELF-SCANNING** at every level of self-creation. (*See Part Six above*) It is essential for you to operate your mind, your bio-computer - the core of your life - *in the holistic unity with your heart, spirit, and consciousness in synch.* Only then will you be able to raise your consciousness to the super level - **Super-Consciousness**. You will accomplish this level of consciousness eventually, if you also tune yourself your **INTUITION,** the inner barometer, which is in fact, the unity of the conscious and sub-conscious minds. Also, start interpreting *meaningful coincidences* that are signs from the Above – the network of the Universal Intelligence that is embracing us everywhere.

Respect your inner voice, rely on it, and trust it!

Tune Yourself up to the Station God!

6. Spirituality is Our Healing Modality!

I have indicated above that *spiritualized intelligence* that you need to attain by this level means *consistent self-work and moral discipline*. Just regular trips to a church on Sundays can hardly be enough for spiritual enrichment. A lot of self-education and self-transformation are needed. Just saying, "*God bless you!*" to passers-by and mechanically repeating the messages from the Bible after the priest will not ascend you to self-salvation. The mental level of the connection with God that you need to attain, must be conquered, and you do need to establish a mental connection with the Universal Informational Field, or the Universal Intelligence on your own, whether you admit it or not.

Raise the voltage of your intelligence and spirit; you are infinite!

1. A spiritually-mature person is very educated, extremely disciplined, very kind, compassionate, forgiving and giving. He is developing these qualities all his life through trial and error, through troubles and tribulations, through moral persistence and deep, unshakable faith. He / she has the right to declare:

I am One with everything under the Sun!

2. Also, be mindful of the necessity to interpret the divine books on our own, applying your own intelligence to the understanding of the insightful messages that are communicated to you, without relying on a priest or any person that is enthusiastic enough to share his brains with you. Be spiritually self-reliant, too.

I am Free to be the Best of Me!

3. What a person digests mentally, having processed the spiritual information through his own experience in bone, is what he will assimilate in flesh. Leo Tolstoy, who was a **true spiritual aristocrat** and a great world-known Russian writer, wrote in his story "*What Men Live By*," "*One may live and develop without a father and a mother, but one cannot live without God that dwells within men and illuminates their souls*".

4. Other than that, we all need **spiritual food of love** that we inherit from our parents Becoming more spiritual, or heightening the level of your spiritual intelligence, you will become much more appreciative of love and the choices that you make, looking for love. Richard Wetherill, the author of a very insightful book "*Right is Might!*" writes,

> "*A man has two ways to go - to evolve or to destroy himself - the choice is his and whatever the choice, there will be the point of no return either way.*"

5. These great words demonstrate that once we choose the right direction, we should never turn back and nothing should have power over us in our determination to pursue the right path in life. Therefore, *conscious praying* is an indispensable part of your growth. *It is your mental and physical nutrition* that your brain produces, *energizing every cell in the body with health and vitality*. Praying and intuition helps us keep *council only with ourselves* and rely on our own judgement and innermost wisdom to keep the inner weather sunny.

"Imitation is human, creation is divine!" (Dalai Lama)

6. Spiritual maturity that you are to gain by this stage will manifest itself in your better reasoning *in terms of the cause-effect strategy of life,* its fundamental Universal Law of Causality. Always start tracing your own or another's behavior to its cause. Eliminating the cause, you change the consequences of your wrong perception of yourself and another person. The whole field of life in its spiritual essence can be glorified by consciously taking care of your own and some one's being with conscious praying.

7. You will become *more aware of the presence of other people in your life*, and you will be more conscious of the fact that people always grade you for your personal quality. Your personal informational electro-magnetic field is either magnetizing them with your charm or drives them away. So, remind yourself auto-suggestively:

Be nice and beautiful and beware, there are eyes and ears everywhere!

8. Mind you, please, you absolutely and unapologetically need *to stop judging other people and start focusing on developing your own light,* giving another person a chance to radiate his or hers in return. We are changing ourselves and the world by changing the way we perceive it, think about it, and talk about it.

It's real spirituality in action! Shine and let others shine, too!

9. Finally, *navigate yourself "on the path of righteousness"*, steer your course, adjust it to the turbulent currents of life, *have private sessions with your conscience,* but do not change the destination of being and becoming - the ultimate reality of you, **the *Ultimate Best of You – the Vintage You*,** *the* one who oversees his thoughts, words, actions, and his soul.

A Soul lives on Spiritual Nutrition!
Are you There Yet?

7. You Are Your Own Church!

There are many wonderfully godly people, real **God–transmitters** in our churches, on TV, on the Internet, and just around us. Some of these people are amazingly insightful and self-educated, to begin with, and therefore, they gather thousands of people that tune to them physically, emotionally, mentally, and spiritually because their mental and spiritual frequencies synchronize with the God's messages. The crowds **Joel Osteen and Joyce Myer** gather are all there to get inspired by the intelligent minds and pure souls that Joel and Joyce preserve in this challenging world against all odds. That's real *spiritual intelligence* that is God-processed and verified,

"I want to know the God's thoughts. The rest is details! (Albert Einstein)

Note please, that just praying is essential only when it is consciously mind-channeled and in no way mechanical. Most spiritually- intelligent people do not interpret God in a scary way of an inevitable punishment for a sinful life. They transmit God, *tuning every listener to the station "God" individually* because it is everyone's personal responsibility to try and find God for themselves. A person should reason out on his/ her own the concepts of the religious manuals he / she is following, without anyone's interpretation to declare, like Jesus Christ.

"I am my Own Church!"

The Universal Informational Field of life, as the creative source, is sorting people out from its direct line because they are like weeds that are supposed to be rooted out. An individual level of the perception of the world, *the selection and organization* of the information that the new time provides become the basis for the holistic spirituality formation for those that are truly intelligent and life-aware.

"Do everything in the spirit of truth – and build it in your own self! Mind is the builder of consciousness and your spirituality". (Derick Prince)

There is another aspect to it. With spiritual maturation, we do not just declare our oneness with the environment - the Sun, the wind, the air, the water, and all living creatures on Earth, we get overwhelmed with this unity. It is a new, enriched, reasoned out love of life that connects the heart and the mind forever.

On My Inner Porch, I am My Own Church!

I am No longer Automatic;

I Am Spiritually-Aristocratic!

8. Spiritual Luminosity

When people of true faith, of a great inner integrity and personal wealth are preaching, they truly " *practice what they preach*" because they have accomplished the self-salvation level. They have attained spiritual maturity!

They become our spiritual luminaries!

Following the luminaries in your life and, going along the path of spiritual salvation, you, too, will finally harmonize your life and get it in synch with ***the Universal Accords of Life,*** changing the melody in our hearts from chaos and disbelief, fear, and insecurity to much more harmonious vibrations. Harmony will manifest itself in your balanced attitude to life and its tribulations, your appearance, and your relationships. You will be becoming more and more whole and able to experience *the uniformity with all forms of life,* harmonizing ourselves from within and radiating happiness back to the world. We are promised to obtain this skill sometime in *the Golden Age of the humanity*, but why not now, in our very limited time - space continuum?

Note it, please, love plays the vital role at the level of self-salvation or spiritual maturation. ***Love permeates all the levels of our soul-refining and self-consciousness growth.*** You get imbued with love for oneself, the loved ones, friends, colleagues, company you work for, the country you live in, the nature, its living beings, the people at large and the world. It seems to be far-fetched, but it's not because only spiritualized love generates in us the state of overwhelming inner grace and luminosity.

Love is literally our spiritual food!

Love is the air that fills up the time-space balloons of our lives with *the electro-magnetic energy, our life-force.* Each fight, the burst of anger, unfaithfulness, tongue-lashing, unkindness, love abuse and lack of control over negative emotions make a prick in the balloon the size of the tip of a needle. The air of love-energy starts blowing out of these tiny holes gradually, but surely, depleting us of the life-force and leaving just an empty piece of the balloon's remnants.

Like the *"Shagreen Skin"* in the famous novel by Honore de Balzac, life will shrink, leaving you unrealized, vexed, and wishful that you had lived it differently. So, follow the advice of a great philosopher, Arthur Schopenhauer,

"Obtain the Connected Consciousness with all,"

And Be Sure to Self-Install!

9. Rationalize Your Life, Thrive!

In practical terms, attaining spiritualized intelligence means *taking conscious control of the subconscious mind,* which is complex and irrational. Working on your holistic self-image and molding yourself in this direction, you are helping the conscious mind take charge of your sub-conscious one that rules your life and turns on your automatic self-drive now and then. Don't ever stop paying aware attention to life! Be rational!

As I have indicated in the Introduction, the first goal on the path of self-installation in life is to ultimately come to the level of self-salvation and develop *the Super-Conscious mind* that will be merging with the Universal Intelligence.

Body + Spirit +Mmind + Consciousness+ Sub-Consciousness + Super-Consciousness!

It is our evolutionary goal, and we need to be achieving it consciously by creating ourselves on this path and enacting this innate ability in us. Gradually, you will establish *a true "connection" with your body, spirit, mind and consciousness* at your own accord, and, most importantly, you will experience the Oneness with life on earth and your unbreakable connection to the universe. The Master Computer is programming your biological computer continuously and everywhere. Your awareness of its work and the ability to tap it for necessary data is what you will be developing at this level. There are many most advanced people on earth who have accomplished this goal.

Knowledge becomes true power only on the spiritual path.

That's why we call the people demonstrating such knowledge sages. For instance, I get completely mesmerized, listening to Drunvalo Melchizedek, one of the greatest sages of our time. All his books are the mine of information and incredible wisdom. They inspire us to know more and more because, like Socrates. we have to say,"

I know that I know nothing; the rest don't know even that."

All we know is that we are supposed to unite our *Heavenly Father's* positively charged energy with the negatively-charged one that *Mother Earth* emanates to be unified as *One living entity* in the most beautiful cosmic infinity.

Beauty is Me; Beauty is My Philosophy!

I often think what life would be like in twenty years or so, and I am dying to live that long. In fact, it's my incentive to write this book and tell you about it.

The Voltage of My Spirit is High and Infinite!

10. Intuition is the Soul's Fruition

The self-development process that is continuous and integrated channels you toward having *a holistic vision of life and acute intuition.* The ability to take prompted by the intuition action is the basis for successful life-style, and it is also an indication of the level of your conscious perception of life. Intuition is your inner voice, your essence, your core, but, like any skill, i***ntuition needs to be trained at all the level*** because it is the result of your growing "*intellectualized spirituality"* and a much higher level of self-consciousness.

With new, holistically-trained "*intellectualized spirituality'*, you will develop *a* new conscious responding to life challenges and take them as a matter of course because they are just magnetic life fluctuations of the Universal Informational Field. You will attract people that have the same gravitational force in their minds and become much more loving and appreciative of the gift of life.

You'll become Living Intelligence in action!

The holographic nature of the Universe and the mind have the structure in which every part reflects the entire Universal Informational Field. If our consciousness reflects accumulated knowledge and processes it in our consciousness, the sub-conscious mind reflects the Universal Informational Field holistically, too.

Our sub-consciousness contains the answers to any question asked and the solution to any problem that we might confront because it is the storage of the universal knowledge first and then the reflection of the personal one. Any problem gets processed through this storage of knowledge - different life events, their outcomes, etc., and, finally, the sub-conscious mind comes up with the solution.

As a matter of fact, our sub-conscious mind is mostly equipped to prompt us the best solutions of any problem, and its tool is consciousness. It becomes your most intimate friend that you can rely on in any situation, if you think consciously and stick to the holistic unity of both hemispheres, tuning to your intuition.

I can…! I want to…! And I will…!

Just a simple conscious repeating of the inspirational booster will enhance *the vibrations of the mind* and wake up your intuition. Your positive input will magnetize the positive out-put, and your intuition will post it on the screen of your mind and heart in their inseparable unity.

Trust your Interior Guts and consult Your Insights!

11. The Ultimate Result Vision of the Best of You!

At the highest point of self-development, everything will melt into one. ***The Ultimate Result Vision** of the best of you (Your URV, See Part two Ch. 12))* or ***the Best of You** image* will be replaced by a real person that will eventually become the Integral You, able to proudly declare:

I am the best of me! I am as good as I could ever be!

As John Barnes, the author of an incredibly mind-enriching book "The ***Stellar Man***" predicts the best of us will become ***the Star People*** in the unforeseeable future. We'll respect life at large. becoming One with the immortal spirit of Universal Intelligence which is God!

The Universal intelligence, therefore, means making your mind-body obey your will which is God's will.

What an uplifting feeling that is! You will build up your inner fortress, ***your personal magnetic core*** that will help you sustain any life trouble. You'll become a man / woman of spiritual, not material quality. The self-induction of the formula of strength will always be energizing, navigating, and calming.

I can, I want to, and I will!

Its inductive power is immense! So, keep internalizing and energizing your becoming a Star person with the help of God. The basic thing for you is to continue doing self-hypnosis consistently as a boost for the self-image and the nourishment for the will-power. Self-hypnosis helps synchronize thoughts and emotions and reeducate the process of thinking and feeling, making you ***a whole human being of intellectualized spirituality.***

Let me be honest with you here. Writing this book, I feel naïve and doubtful that anyone will ever consider these wisdoms worth reading, still more so, following. The world around me is so corrupt, impersonal, immoral, and sarcastically-negative that to have the notion that personality formation can be taken seriously by anyone seems to be an illusion. It's like living under the socialist social system that was all rotten and believe blindly that we were building communism.

However, if we stop dreaming and believing in the possibility of a human race not only to develop technologically, but emotionally, mentally, and spiritually, we will become dead souls with a piece of never melting ice in the hearts.

"The Way for us is to Be the Way!"

(Neal Donald Walsch)

12. Envision a Better Scenario of Your Life -Thrive!

In sum, to have a better life, we absolutely need *to train our imagery and our positive thinking*. Like anything else, positive thinking needs conscious training to be able to master the subconscious mind that records all our bad patterns of behavior, emotional disturbances, and other negative occurrences in life. Let me continue assuring you that eventually, you will learn *to think consequentially, not impulsively* because your conscious assessment of the self-reality will get synchronized with new frequencies of intelligence and consciousness.

The textuality of your personality will be focused on infinity!

Naturally, to put an end to the negative current, you need to have many good, positive ones recorded by the subconscious mind. Fry to enlarge the number of good deed and reserved responses to life. You will overpower your *impulsiveness* and automatic reactions consciously with the" *Halt*" command.

It takes only a stroke to change a minus into a plus!

By the same token, you can imagine a much better scenario of your whole life. Upload it into your mind with the help of the induction *I can…; I want to…; and I will…!* Enjoy watching the success-movies of different life outcomes during your auto- suggestive meditation, when lying flat on the floor at home, on the beach, or taking a solo break at work. Smile while watching the movie. Download the movie into every cell of your brain and the body. Remember, your AUTO–MEDIA is constantly at your service, and it will provide the most uplifting scenarios and inspirational stories of the continuation of your life. Keep training your auto-media auto-suggestively:

Life is tough; (Breathe in) / but I am tougher! (Breathe out)

My whines and tears, smiles and fears will all vanish (Breathe in), as the evolutionary garnish! (Breathe out)

I never whine; (Breathe in) I shine! (Breathe out)

I am a New Me; (Breathe in) I am a Better Me! (Breathe out)

Life is going on (Breathe in), and it is beautiful! (Breathe out)

I am happy no matter what! (in) Happiness is my full-time job! (out)

Only with God in Synch Am I What I Think!

13. We are all in the Court of the Almighty God!

Self-salvation is also the stage of a highly developed self-conscience in a person. Conscience is literally our direct line with God. Also, **conscience is the core of the mental-emotional grid.** Conscience and intuition are inseparable entities. They are testing every thought we have, every uncontrolled word we say, and every automatic action we take. What we call a guilt–trip is, in fact, an uneasy feeling that is always crashing us after any wrong doing. It is conscience at work.

To keep yourself unspotted, you need to use the scanning mechanism of the cause-effect frame-work of the mind-heart unanimity and do it before taking an unconscious, reactive, and uncontrolled action. Conscience is, no doubt, the propelling mechanism of your self-development, too, because it is connected to the magnetic core of your *"the Flower of Life," the Merkabah*, or the sacred formation grid of your soul. (*Dundalk Melchizedek*) Conscience is also the testing mechanism of your growing self- consciousness, governed by your tuning to the station "God" continuously for intuitive self-assessment and guidance.

I tune myself to the station God for His everlasting support!

Naturally, having attained the stage of self-salvation does not guarantee you from sliding up again to the mini level of self-formation and self-installation. The virus of self-destruction can get into your biological compute at any time, and therefore, *you need to be vigilant not to ever be victimized* by any biological or artificial mind!

Non- victimization

Is my inner salvation!

I don't let you or any Boss
To ever turn me into a human Moth!

Nor do I allow anyone to delete

The spark of my divine It!

I have in Me

A very special Glee!

I train my brain for it to sustain

The range of my every day change!

No Victimization is My Salvation!

14. The Auto-Suggestive Meditation

As I have suggested above, you need to connect your breathing to inspirational inducting to enhance the boosting effect of the Auto-Suggestive meditation that should become the part of your inner life. Breathe in, inducting the beginning of the mind-set *(an authoritative statement here)*, make a pause, internalizing its concept, and breathe out, reasoning the end of the induction. Keep the holistic paradigm always in mind.

Synthesis – Analysis - Synthesis!

When you do the inducting of just one booster, for instance," ***In my life quest, I am the best"!*** say it three times, accompanying it by deep breathing. You will immediately feel the influx of energy and the determination to overcome any difficulty on your way.

Language is a dynamic interplay of consciousness!

The quality of your life depends on the quality of your thoughts and ***the quality of the words that frame your thoughts.*** They must be in synch. So, don't ever be casual with your language. It's the greatest gift of God. Thus, you will be able to establish a fresh connection with the subconscious mind.

It is your best friend; it's your beginning and your end!

We know now that the left hemisphere of the brain *(men's side)* is negatively charged and is governed by logic. The right hemisphere of the brain *(women's side)* is positively charged, and it is responsible for intuition. Women are known to have much better developed intuitions than men, and therefore, woman are much more evolved creatures. Women more than men **have their hearts and minds in synch.** A well-known saying below takes a whole new meaning:

Behind every successful man is a woman!

At any level of your self-salvation, you need to expand the right brain's creative potential, putting the two brains in synch. The whole brain joint potential will reward you with much richer intuition and ***telepathic abilities of* MIND-TO-MIND** and **MIND-TO-HEART** telepathic communication of the future.

Our mind and heart mending is never ending!

Auto-Induction:

I Am a Sage on My Personal Stage!

15. I Never Whine; I Shine!

Continue to do suggestive inspiring in the open air, too. **Unite with the Universal Intelligence** every time you are outside in the Sun, looking up into the clouds. Try to decipher their messages for yourself. Be full of gratitude, when you are enjoying the view of the night sky. Connect to the distant stars, emanating their mind-boggling intelligence to us. Feel mesmerized with their beauty. **See yourself, surrounded by light,** immersing you in its luminous substance when your mood sags, when you feel sick, or need more energy. The Sun rays, the light of the stars, or even the light of every lamp you are passing while driving will do you a lot of good if you learn to appreciate light overall. Here is a simple *auto-suggestive verse* that I use when I am overwhelmed with the beauty of life or its chaos.

Dear God Sun, Ra!

I am one of Your rays,

You are in my time and my space!

With You in me,

I am full of spiritual glee!

With You in my heart and the mind,

I am ready to unwind

All the problems in front of me and behind!

If you happen to be walking, **breathe consciously at every step,** saying this auto-induction with much gratitude and love. Facing the Sun, breathe in light, love, peace, and harmony; breathe out darkness, discord, and disharmony. Make light-filling self-work your second nature. Radiate light yourself!

I never whine; I shine!

After you have enlightened the consciousness of your body, you can start purifying it on **the cellular level**, heightening your aware attention to the body's needs and its "complaints" to you in the form of pain, fatigue, depression, sadness, disappointment, inner emptiness and loneliness, as I have described above. **Always unify your body, spirit, mind, and self-consciousness.**

Give Your Consciousness a Much Better Home to Operate from!

16. Make Your Heart Smart, and the Mind Kind!

***Learn to deal
with the verbs
to love, to give, and to forgive
before you actually, leave
The Tree of Life
as its precious Leaf!***

It'll Come to Me Intuitively!

**Let's Take Life from the Gutters because
All Life Matters!**

17. Don't Be Life-Negligent; Be Life-Intelligent!

Sharpen and Focus Your Aware Attention To Get to a Higher Spiritual Dimension!

Self-Induction:

My Self-Salvation is in Inner Maturation!

18. For the Reader to Consider

The Fifth Stage of Spiritual Maturation and Soul Refinement

In sum, having raised your *self-awareness, established your constant self-monitoring, enriched holistically your general intelligence, realized your unique professional potential, and raised substantially your self-consciousness*. *Be* sure to boost your spirit with the first accomplishment *at the super-level (universal)* of your personality-formation and self-creation.

The Route of Self-Resurrection:

Universal Connection	**Self-Salvation**	*Universal Dimension*
Spiritual Maturity	**Self-Realization**	*Spiritual Dimension*
Mental Awareness	**Self-Installation**	*Mental Dimension*
Emotional Control	**Self-Monitoring**	*Emotional Dimension*
Physical Fitness	**Self-Knowledge**	*Physical Dimension*

I admit - I am physically-fit!

I admit - I am emotionally -fit!

I admit - I am mentally-fit!

I admit - I am spiritually-fit!

I admit - I am universally fit!

I am a Better Me! I am as Good as I Could Ever Be!

Conclusion

I Am the Whole Me; I am the Best I could Ever Be!

"To love oneself is the beginning of a life-long romance."
(Oscar Wilde)

**I Program Myself on the Pulse:
A Happy, Happy, Happy Life Waltz!**

I am Moving Forward, Onward, God-ward;

What is Your Direction Toward?

1. I am Flying Like an Angel Over the Chaos of the World!

My thoughts are bright,
My body is light!
My future is full of glory;
My presence is devoid of folly!
I follow my ways
And accomplish my life's surveys
Toward the glorious Sun
And the fabulous Moon,
Toward the goals I want
To attain soon!

I Have Stoicism, Grace, and Humility.
I Am the Personality!

2. Being the Best is a Life-Long Quest!

In conclusion, let's summarize the most important concepts of the book. Every person seeks to satisfy his / her internal hunger for the solution of their daily problems and get the answer to the questions why they are suffering, to begin with, and what they are here for.

To answer these questions, you need to take the light side of life every moment and stay there, no matter what, adding your own energy to ***the Universal Energy Field*** that sustains your ***physical, emotional, mental, spiritual, and universal well-being on Earth*** and helps you battle the darkness of ignorance, lack of morals, personal de-magnetization, and soul destruction.

The holistic perception of life, the methodology of which I have presented above, demands a ***lot of self-education and developed self-consciousness,*** the consciousness at which you comprehend the total unity of everything, become more aware of the essence of life in the Universe, and actively contribute your own tiny bit to it with a great sense of responsibility for every human contact you might have on your life path.

Every human contact is a responsibility!

We need to learn ***to live consciously*** and work out ***a strategic path of action***, on the one hand, and ***an individualized recipe*** for each disturbed soul, on the other. Your soul needs to acquire a lot of self-knowledge and go through self-monitoring, self-installment, and self-realization before it attains self-salvation.

This book is an attempt to present such ***plan of action***, and you are free to choose what points of this plan fit your aspirations to become a personable, charismatic, noble, and accomplished human being.

I have tried to help you obtain ***your innate wholeness of the body, spirit, mind, soul, and consciousness*** to be able to raise your **SELF-CONSCIOUSNESS**, filling up your unique vessel of life with ***the Living Skills*** to finally channel your life toward spiritual self-salvation.

However, these qualities do not come on their own unless you work consistently and willfully on developing them. I suggest doing it with the help of the self-inductions that are meant to back your spirit up on your most vital path.

Self-Induction:

Spiritual Maturation is My Self-Salvation!

3. There Are No Limits to Perfection!

In sum, there are *eighteen self-inductions* that I consider to be most important for your self-monitoring and personality growth. Pick the ones that might help you *strategize your life,* download them to your biological computer, and keep the rest in your mind's storage. Monitor your breathing. Breathe in when saying inwardly the first part of the induction. Make a short pause, instilling it to your conscious mind. Breathe out, inducting the second part if the inspirational booster. Relax. Repeat it. It's never enough to self-induct this stuff. You can adorn them into a much more willful form, too.

I can…! I want to….! And I will…!

1. *Expand your life awareness without laziness!*
2. *Envision everything you do with precision!*
3. *Mean what you say and say what you mean!*
4. *Do not apply too much eloquence; apply patience and tolerance.*
5. *Intolerance raises the blood pressure permanence!*
6. *Conduct a self-limitation war – less is more!*
7. *Do not hurt, not to be hurt in an evil reward!*
8. *Do not dirty anyone's life to keep yours clean inside.*
9. *Stay in the financial intelligence flow; make your expenses low!*
10. *Have an unbeatable confidence and strength at length!*
11. *Turn a self-destructive mechanism into a self-constructive optimism!*
12. *Be resilient and self-reliant; be patient, inspirational and kind!*
13. *Don't magnetize the problem's size!*
14. *Don't say "yes" when you mean "No!"*
15. *Life has no value if the soul is devalued!*
16. *Don't be reliant on people! Rely on God and stay in His Fort!*
17. *Be addicted to life! Pray it, drink it, and Thrive!*

"We cannot Live Better than in Seeking to Become Better!" *(Socrates)*

4. The Vintage Me is All You Should See!

Constructing *the Best of Me self - image*, you are developing your **spiritual maturity**, or your spiritual wellness which means that you are getting in control of your conscious and subconscious mind under the super-conscious mind.

Body +Mind + Spirit + Self-Consciousness+ Super Consciousness!

(subconscious mind + conscious mind)

These qualities are essential. You could benefit from what you have learned and use the information for any one's personal installation. You might have noticed the use of the verbs **must** and **should** in my text that I tried to make as objective as possible. But the computer wouldn't let me us e the modal structure **"have to."** It continuously made me change it into **must or should,** anyway.

Everyone has a calling *to begin his / her persona quest* and discover who he / she is. Nobody is looking at the whole picture, though. What really matters is having a healthy professional life, expressing yourself creatively, being stable financially, and being spiritually connected. So, listen to your inner guts and see where your intuition channels you along these paths. Consider the validity of every thought in this book for your personal good and the necessity for any transformation.

Intuition is the divine spark in you!

It leads you along the path of spiritual maturation in any situation. It guides, it heals, it connects you to the Universal Informational Field that is the best councilor you can ever get.

Conscious *perception* of the information that the Universal Informational Field is emitting to us, its *selection and organization,* backed up by cause+ effect reasoning, and, finally, your aware *strategizing your life* will make a qualitative change in it and upgrade you Spiritual Salvation.

I have put a Lot of Zest into Being the Best!

When you empower yourself with *the Art of Living,* you will be having the same vibrational frequencies with the universe. Many advanced souls have already developed such ability on the earth. it is called *the Kundalini Vibrations*. Your spiritual awareness will result in the achievement of *spiritual maturation*, and you will start experiencing the Divine flow of universal intelligence within.

Consciousness is what results from growth, and all growth is educational.

Constantly working on our intelligence at five levels outlined above, you will be able, like Prometheus, bring light to people and become *an enlightened being* yourself.

Naturally, you can develop *your own Know-How of self-creation,* in which knowledge and skills will be in one unity with *the form and content* of your life.

Of course, such aware attention to your life requires commitment, discipline, and a tremendous will-power. But what a rewarding feeling it is to be guided in life with knowledge and self-developed Living Skills.

You've become wise and able to self-advise!

You develop an unbeatable spirit, strong enough to dictate to your sub-conscious mind to erase the scars of the past and take full responsibility of the present. Both of your brains will work in synch and you *will create a strong psychic synergy* to declare:

I Am Free to Be the Best of Me!

I am working at my inner glee, I'm becoming a Luminary!

I am getting into the state of physical, emotional, mental, spiritual, and universal equilibrium. I am positive. I am not too materialistic!

I am spiritually -aristocratic!

I am not lazy to think. I am disciplined in my thoughts, words, emotions, actions, attitudes, morals, my eating, my breathing, and my everyday living.

I synergize my life. I do not attribute everything to chance. I monitor my life! I am an enlightened, advanced, spiritual human being.

"I take care of the Outside for People;
I take care of the Inside for God!'

(Edgar Cayce)

5. The Law of Reap and Sow is on the Go!

Having read the book and internalized the holistically- constructive ideas of self-creation, I am sure that *the Law of Reap and Sow* will get manifested in you.

We are never at rest! We are on the spiritual quest!

You have managed to plant the seed of your *"intellectually-spiritualized" personality* into your *Magnetic Circuit of life,* your Personal Informational Electro-Magnetic Field, and you can reap the result and rightfully declare:

I know who I am!

I am a strong, calm, and determined owner of my free will,

I can be personable! I want to be personable!

I have become personable!

Congratulations!

You have justified your own expectations!

Self-Induction:

I Can Roam Any Terrain with God in My Vein!

6. Final Self-Induction:

Let the light of God
Be reflected in my face;
Let the wisdom of God
Be reflected in my faith!

        Let the accuracy of God
        Be reflected in my outreach;
        Let the precision of God
        Be reflected in my tone pitch!

Let the love of God
Be reflected in my actions;
Let the attitude of God
Be reflected in my reactions!

        Let the beauty of God
        Be reflected in my looks;
        Let the perfection of God
        Be Reflected in my moods!

Only then May God release me into the Life Stream
As Perfect as His Creation Seam!

7. Nothing is Impossible for Anyone Personable!

Life is Going on, and it is Worth My having been Born!

I Am Free to Be the Best of Me!

I Make Love Elation My Inner Creation!

I Accept My Life in Its Entire Mass, For It, too, Shall Pass!

Post Thought!

"Go Beyond, Fully Beyond, Completely Beyond!"

The Soul-Installation Track is Not Crowded For Those who are Holistically-Rounded!

Nothing is Impossible

If Your Dreams are Irreversible!

1. "I Have a Dream!" *(Martin Luther King Jr.)*

When we arrived in the USA, there were many things that we lacked in the former Soviet Union of those destructive times, but the country of plenty lacked one thing that my 13-year old daughter noticed very soon and told me one day after she came home from Mamaroneck School. in Westchester.

-"Mom, I know my dream now. I will start a business in this country; **I will build the center for kids!** *They have no Pioneer Canters for kids, where I learnt folk-dancing, ballet-dancing, sewing, fishing, swimming, space-flying, and toy-making.* **Poor kids. They don't have that here. Nor do they have anything for teenagers. What should I do here? Where do I go after school?** *My school peers talk only about parties, bars sex ,and sleep-overs".*

I was glad that she started thinking in the American way business-wise, but I was truly upset that she was right about the second part of her observation that very soon became a true nightmare for me. The reality changed her dream, and even though she became a computer-designer and got four books for kids published, she did not manage *to bridge her dream and the reality and become totally self-realized.* She had never spoken about it again.

Years went by, but I have never forgotten that conversation and the spark in Yolanda's eyes because I saw the same spark in the eyes of many of my students whom I try to inspire to never betray their dreams and become what they aspire to be, not what just secures their life As a matter of fact, *my five books on self-awareness, self-monitoring, self-installation, self-realization, and self-salvation* in life, are inspired by my daughter's unrealized dream to have the center like **that here and, possibly, in other countries of the world.**

My dream is to have *a free center* **"JUPITER"** that will be structured in five rings - *physical, emotional, mental, spiritual, and universal*, opening the doors to **FIVE SPACE STATIONS:**

5. Universal Space Station
4. Spiritual Space Station
3. Mental Space Station
2. Emotional Space Station
1. Physical Space Station

Wouldn't it be great to have the **PSYSICAL SPACE STATION** for the kids and teenagers where they will be developing their physical abilities, like it was in the ancient Greek school for Spartans. They will have a chance to enrich their *cognitive skills* and learn many new interesting things of their choice, as well as train their *digital skills* in the most creative ways. *(the book "I am Free to Be the Best of Me!")*

Next, at the **EMOTIONAL STACE STATION** , the kids will learn about an array of beautiful human emotions and how to handle their Amygdala gland with the help of the best movies, tales, works of art, and beautiful classic music There will be instructors – *psychologists- emotionalists* and *robot - friends* to back them up if they happen to swoon emotionally. *(the book "Soul-Refining")*

THE CHOICES WE MAKE DICTATE THE LIFE WE LIVE!

The holistic pyramid of essential *Vistas of Intelligence* will be at their fingerprints when they chose to spiral up to the **MENTAL SPACE STATION** to fill up the gaps in the levels of intelligence that this book features. They will enhance their awareness by connecting their two brains and boosting their creativity and ascertaining their dream of what they want to become *(the book "Living Intelligence or the Art of Becoming!")*

The most inspiring knowledge of the human evolutionary *spiritual growth* will await them at the **SPIRITUAL SPACE,** with no preaching or religious indoctrination, but insightful, interesting enlightening the minds to shape their *spiritualized intelligence.(the book "Self-Taming!")*

The space-time journey into the impossible will complete at the **UNIVERSAL SPACE STATION,** with breath-taking make-belief flight of imagination in *the top observatory + a virtual space* station that will take them on interstellar travels into space. *(the book "Beyond the Terrestrial!)*

And the best thing of all - there will be no obligations , no words: *"You are supposed to…"/ "You need to pay first!" That's not your station!" You need to first do this…"*

The possibilities are limitless, as well as our incredible NOW

that is, in fact, our wonderous future!

Long Live the Beat of "So Be It!"

Dr. Rimaletta Ray with her Inspirational Say!

*1. "**Emotional Diplomacy** or **Follow the Bliss of the Uncatchable Is!**"/ **Editorial** LEIRIS, New York, USA, 2010*

*2. "**Four Dimensions of a Soul**" (Auto-Suggestive Psychology in Russian) / LEIRIS Publishing, New York, USA, 2011*

*3. "**Americanize Your Language, Emotionalize Your Speech!**" / Nova Press, USA, 2011*

*4. "**It Too Shall Pass!**" (Inspirational Boosters in Four Dimensions) / Xlibris, 2012*

*5. "**I am Strong in My Spirit!**" (Inspirational Boosters in Russian) / Xlibris, 2013*

*6. "**Language Intelligence or Universal English**" (Method of the Right Language Behavior), **Book One** /Xlibris, 2013*

*7. "**Language Intelligence or Universal English**" (Remedy Your Language Habits," **Book Two** /Xlibris, 2013*

*8. "**Language Intelligence or Universal English**," (Remedy Your Speech Skills) **Book Three** /Xlibris, 2013*

*9. "**Living Intelligence or the Art of Becoming**" (A New Paradigm of Self-Creation) Xlibris, 2015*

*10. "**My Solar System**," (Auto-Suggestive Psychology for Inner Ecology) Xlibris, 2015*

*11. **Beyond the Terrestrial!** (Be the Station for Self-Inspiration!), Xlibris, June 2016*

*12. **Soul-Refining!** (Toplinkpublishing.com. May 2017)*

*13. "**Self-Taming**" (Book Whip, 2018)*

www. Language – fitness.com / Emotional Diplomacy.com
- rimma143@hotmail.com / Tel. (203) 212-2673
Yolantalensky1979@gmail.com / (203) 850- 4791

www.ingramcontent.com/pod-product-compliance
Lightning Source LLC
Chambersburg PA
CBHW080025130526
44591CB00037B/2669